URALIC AND ALTAIC SERIES

Volume 48

Routledge
Taylor & Francis Group
LONDON AND NEW YORK

The Uralic and Altaic Series
Volumes 1–150, 1960–1990

First published 1997 by Curzon Press Ltd

Published 2022 by Routledge
4 Park Square, Milton Park, Abingdon, Oxon OX14 4RN
605 Third Avenue, New York, NY 10017

Routledge is an imprint of the Taylor & Francis Group, an informa business

Publisher's Note

The publisher has gone to great lengths to ensure the quality of this reprint but points out that some imperfections in the original copies may be apparent.

ISBN 978-0-700-70848-2 (hbk)

CUSTOMARY LAW OF

THE NOMADIC TRIBES OF SIBERIA

CUSTOMARY LAW OF THE NOMADIC TRIBES OF SIBERIA

Indiana University Publications
Uralic and Altaic Series, Vol. 48

by Valentin A. Riasanovsky

Published by Indiana University, Bloomington
Mouton & Co., The Hague, The Netherlands
1965

INDIANA UNIVERSITY PUBLICATIONS

Graduate School

URALIC AND ALTAIC SERIES

Volume 48

Originally published: *Customary Law of the Nomadic Tribes of Siberia*
by Professor V. A. Riasanovsky, Tientsin, 1938.

All orders from the United States of America and from
Canada should be addressed to the
Editor, Uralic and Altaic Series, Patton House,
Indiana University, Bloomington, Indiana

Orders from all other countries should be sent to
Mouton & Co., Publishers, The Hague, The Netherlands

CONTENTS

PREFACE

The present work contains a concise general survey of the customary law of the nomadic tribes of Western and Eastern Siberia (but not of the Far East)[1].

The native tribes mentioned in this survey comprise the main part of the native population of Siberia (without the Far East) and belong to different ethnical groups: Turki, Mongol, Tungus and Urgo-Finnish. The community of the culture of these tribes, based on the clan-patriarchal organization and nomadic economy with the common fundamental institutions of law arising therefrom give us the right for examining their law in common in the present work.

As the customary law of the aforesaid native tribes, in particular the non-Mongolian tribes, is not well investigated, the Author hopes in time to return again to this subject.

August, 1938
Tientsin.

1 Some of the sketches which compose this outline were published earlier in the form of separate articles.

1. JURISTIC CUSTOMS OF THE KIRGHIZ.

Records of Kirghiz Law.

The Kirghiz or Kirghiz-Kaisaks are a nomadic tribe of mixed origin, with Turki elements predominating. At one time they were the subjects of the Mongols and entered into the composition of the Ooloos of Juchi or Golden Horde (XIII-th — XV-th centuries) and partly of the Ooloos of Jagatai. After the decline and fall of the Golden Horde, they formed part of the Uzbek Ooloos (XVI-th century), and finally made up an administration of their own consisting of three hordes, the Greater, Medium and Lesser. During the XVII-th century the Kirghiz-Kaisaks were now in friendly relations with the neighboring Oirats, now at war with them in the East and with the Kalmucks in the West. In the last quarter of this century the Kirghiz tribes were ruled by Khan Tiavka, their best administrator and lawgiver. This sovereign had his residence at Tashkent and ruled all three Kirghiz hordes through his lieutenants placed directly over them. During the first half of the XVIII-th century the Kirghiz were subjected to great pressure by the Oirats and a part of them (the Greater Horde) were actually under Oirat rule. Towards the middle of the XVIII-th century the Kirghiz recognized themselves as subjects of Russia, but for long afterwards they retained a semi-independent status, and it was not until the second quarter of the XIX-th century that one could really speak of the subjection of the majority of them to the dominion of the Russians. This subjection was defined by the "Statute Concerning the Siberian Kirghiz" of 1822, which came into force in the year 1824 and preserved its significance as the basis for the subsequent legislation for the Kirghiz. The Kirghiz-Kaisaks lived and still live chiefly in Siberia and Steppe regions (the Medium and Greater Hordes) and in Eastern Russia where live the Lesser Horde (Orenburg region) and its offshoot, the Bukeiev Horde (in the province of Astrakhan). The total number of Kirghiz (Kirghiz-Kaisaks) at the beginning of the XX-th century was more than 3.000.000 souls,[2] and they thus represent the most numerous of the nomadic tribes of Asia.

2 *v.* Brockhaus-Efron *Encyclopaedic Dictionary,* vol. XXIX, p. 104, *Great Encyclopedia,* vol. X, p. 746 (total population 3.236.000).

Another related group of the same people are the Kara-Kirghiz, the majority of whom live in China and the minority in the U. S. S. R.

According to the Statute concerning the Kirghiz of Siberia of 1822, 50-70 kibitkas composed an Aoul, the Aouls were unified into Volosts (small district), consisting of 10-12 Aouls, and the Volosts into Okrugs (big district), containing 15-20 Volosts. The administration was in the hands of the honoured clan elders. Thus Aouls were ruled by Elders, the Volosts by Sultans, the Okrug—by the Office, consisting of the Chief Sultan as the Head and four Assessors: two Russian and two Kirghiz. The competence of the Aoul's Elders and Sultans consisted of administrative affairs, the Offices of Okrugs had not only administrative authority but also judicial (it consisted of the court of the second and final degree; the first degree was the court of honoured elders-Beys).

At the present time (i.e. since the Russian Revolution of 1917) the territories of the Kara-Kirghiz and Kirghiz-Kaisaks respectively compose the Kirghiz and Kazakh Soviet Socialist Republics.

1. The oldest records of Kirghiz law are the so-called "Laws of Khan Tevka (or Tiavka)". The famous ruler of the Kirghiz, Khan Tevka, codified the ancient customs of his people and added to them several provisions of his own devising. This code has not come down to us in its complete form, but excerpts from it are given by Levshin who lived among the Kirghiz during the years 1820-21 and left us a three-volume work, "A Description of the Kirghiz-Kaisak Hordes and Steppes", 1832. On pp. 170-178 of the third volume, the author quotes 33 fragments of the Code of the Laws of Khan Tevka, consisting of the ancient customs of the Kirghiz (29 fragments) and 4 fragments of the provisions of Khan Tevka. By their contents, the former belong predominantly to the fields of criminal law and court procedure. That these 29 fragments represent the repetition of the ancient customs of the Kirghiz is evident both from their contents and from the evidence of Levshin, who repreduces what he was told by the Kirghiz themselves,[3] as well as from the fact that the mandatory provisions or Khan Tevka are given as a supplement with a special explanation.

2. "The Customs of the Kirghiz" contain 9 chapters and 208 articles. They were complied in 1824 at the demand of the Russian authorities who were then preparing the codification of the customary

3 "The Kirghiz of the Greater and Medium Hordes state that their national laws are much older than Khan Tevka," writes Levshin (*op. cit.*, p. 170).

law of the native tribes of Western and Eastern Siberia. On the basis of the materials thus collected, the Code of Steppe Laws of the Nomadic Tribes of Eastern Siberia (draft) was printed in 1841 but never received legislative confirmation.[4] Materials gathered for this codification on the customary laws of the Siberian natives (or at any rate a part of them) were published by Professor Samokvasov in his "Collection of the Customary Laws of the Siberian Natives", published in 1876. The above-mentioned "Customs of the Kirghiz" comprise pp. 245-282 of this work. They consist of 9 chapters as follows: I. On religious worship; II. On courts and judges; III. On witnesses: IV. On homicide, mayhem, wounds, fights and insults; V. On concealing malefactors and permitting them to escape; VI. On sodomy, rape and lechery; VII. On extortion; VIII On theft; and IX. Concerning lawsuits.

We may now acquaint ourselves with the contents of the abovementioned records of Kirghiz law.

The So-called Laws of Khan Tevka.[5]

1. "The place of first importance is occupied by the *law of retaliation*: for blood, revenge is taken in blood, and for mutilation by similar mutilation." (*Droit du taillon*)

2. "For theft, robbery, violence, adultery, the culprit is to be punished by death,"

"According to these laws the relatives of the victim had the right to put the slayer to death, while a person cutting off an arm, leg, ear, etc., was to be deprived of the corresponding part of his own body. Incidentally, punishments could be mitigated in accordance with the sentences of the judges or with the consent of the plaintiffs, in which case the culprit was punished only by the fine fixed for each crime[6]. A murderer could save his life by the payment of *Koon,* i.e. by giving 1,000 sheep for each murdered men and 500 for each woman. A man mutilating another or depriving him of a limb could in the same way pay a fixed number of animals. A thumb was valued at 100 sheep, a little finger at 20, etc."

---

4 *v.* further, 8th outline.

5 The numbering of the articles is the author's, while the rest is a (translated) recapitulation of the information given by Levshin, *op. cit.*, pp. 170 seq.

6 A law known among all Moslems since it was based on the Koran (Note by Levshin).

3. "Whoever kills a Sultan or a Hodja pays the relatives of his victim Koon for seven men. Insult by word to a Sultan or Hodja is punished by a fine of 9 animals; beating them, by 27 heads of cattle."

4. "If a wife kills her husband, she must immediately be put to death, from which no payment of Koon can save her unless (his) relatives forgive her. Pregnant wives are excluded from the operation of this regulation, these not being punished for the murder of their husbands but forever given over to contempt and considered to be without honour. If a husband kills his wife he can deliver himself from execution by paying half Koon."

5. "Parents were not liable to any penalty for the killing of their children, but if a woman killed her infant begotten in adultery she was put to death."

6. "Suicides are buried separately."

7. "If a woman is knocked down by a mounted man and crippled so that as a result of this she bears a stillborn child, then the offender must pay fines as follows: for a child up to 5 months, a horse for each month; while for children of from 5 to 9 months, for each month a camel."

8. "Rape is considered equivalent to murder, and the offender must be put to death or pay Koon to the husband for a wife and to her relatives for a maiden; however, marriage to a raped maiden with the payment of Kalim for her exempts the offender both from execution and from payment of Koon."

9. "A husband discovering his wife in adultery may kill her, and if he does this immediately after uncovering the crime he is not punished. In any other case he may ask the judges for a sentence of death upon the faithless wife and her tempter if their crime be proved; but if 4 persons of good repute swear their innocence the court must not subject them to any penalty."

10. "The abductor of another's wife without her consent is punished by death or the imposition of Koon; but if the abduction took place with the consent of the woman then the abductor may retain her upon paying the husband Kalim and besides this procuring him a maiden without payment of Kalim."

11. "Anyone insulting a woman must ask her pardon, and if she refuses it he must pay for dishonour."

12. "Incest is punishable by death; but this is substituted by the sentence of the family, since such crimes cannot be submitted for the consideration of outsiders."

13. "A blasphemer accused by seven witnesses must be put to death by stoning."

14 "If anyone is converted to the Christian faith, his relatives may take from him all his property"

15. "Owners have an unlimited power of life and death over their slaves. The complaint of a slave against his master is not heard anywhere."

16. "A son daring to insult or beat his father or mother is seated astride a black cow with his face to its tail, and with pieces of old felt hung around his neck; this cow is led around the Aouls and he that sits on it is beaten. A daughter guilty of the same offence is bound and handed over to her mother for punishment at her will."

17. "Anyone discovered stealing must return what is stolen thrice nine (27) fold, and this punishment is called *Aibana.* If the theft is of cattle, then the culprit must give besides camels, one captive; besides horses, a camel; and besides sheep, a horse. A hundred camels are equal to 300 horses and 1,000 sheep."

18. "Whoever commits murder and theft together must pay for two crimes."

19. "A wife and children knowing of a theft by their husband or father and not reporting it are not subjected to any punishment, since it is not permitted to denounce the elder in a family."

20. "For the killing of a hunting hound or golden eagle the owner may demand a male or female slave."

21. "If a son who has separated himself from his father should die childless, then his property must go to his father. Minor children are given over to the guardianship of the next of kin, and if these be absent, to people of good repute."

22. "Wills are made in the presence of relatives and Mullahs."

23. "Horses, cows and cattle which have been in the hands of others are recovered with whatever increase there is, except in the case of cattle driven away as *Barantu.* To certify that there has been no concealment, the oath of the possessor is demanded."

24. "Disputes must be settled and sentence on them passed if not by the Khan himself then by the administrators or elders of

those Aouls to which the plaintiff and defendant belong with the participation of two invited arbitrators appointed one by each side."

25. "If a plaintiff suspects any of the judges he may set them aside."

26. "If a defendant does not answer a court summons or a sentenced person cannot pay his fine, the latter is collected from his relatives or from his Aoul, these having the right to compensate themselves for their losses by the execution upon the culprit of the sentence of the court."

27. "For the establishment of a crime not less than two and sometimes three witnesses are required. In the absence of witnesses it is permitted to resort to the oath, but neither the defendant nor the plaintiff shall be permitted to swear for themselves and there must swear for them persons known for their honesty. If no one is found to swear for an accused person he is considered guilty. Persons of the female sex, like workers, servants and slaves, are not admitted as witnesses."

28. "For deciding litigations, judges and arbitrators are to be compensated by one tenth of the amount involved in the suit."

29. "If a sentenced person does not carry out the sentence of a judge, or the Headman of an Aoul purposely avoids considering a case and thus protects a criminal, then the plaintiff receives the right, with the permission of his elder, to perform *Barantu,* i.e. to go to the Aoul of the defendant with his own relatives or nearest neighbours and secretly drive away his cattle to his own home. However, upon returning home he must report this to his Headman who sees to it that the amount of the compensation is commensurate with the amount of the suit."

In addition to the articles reproduced above, Levshin reported the following provisions promulgated by Khan Tevka:

30. "The Khan himself, and also all the Sultans, elders and administrators, must gather each autumn at a certain place in the middle of the steppe for the discussion of the affairs of the people."

31. "No Kirghiz must ride to the assembly of the people otherwise than with his arms. Persons without arms have no vote and their juniors may not yield them their places."

32. "Every man capable of bearing arms (except Sultans) must pay the Khan and administrators as a tax a twentieth of his property every year."

33. "Each generation, clan, and division must have its own *Tamga* (sign serving as an emblem). These Tamgas are distributed and they must be stamped on all cattle and property so that all may distinguish what belongs to whom."

Contents of the Customs of the Kirghiz, Codified in 1824.
Private Law.

Property law. — The land was held for use by clan-unions for purposes of nomadic cattle-breeding, "Whoever shall, with camp or cattle, occupy the lands of others, shall be driven from the spot; and the overseers shall be beaten" (C. of Kir., 168). Whoever shall take possession of the land of others, from him shall it be taken away even after 15 years have passed (*Ibid.*, 188). The right of property in movables was recognized (*Ibid.*, 166, 181, 189, etc.).

Anyone finding a lost thing or cattle must report it to his relatives or the Volost (district) authorities and shall receive ¼ of the lost things or ⅛ of the cattle or whatever the master may give. But if he shall hide his discovery he shall be considered without honour and not received in society (*Ibid.*, 156, 157). If a pledge is not redeemed by the set time and exceeds in value the sum received, then the pledge-holder receives from it the sum due him, the remainder of the pledge being returned to the pledge-giver; if, however, the pledge is of less value that the sum of the debt, then the pledge-giver (debtor) must pay the remainder (165). Should the pledge-holder damage the pledge through neglect, he must return its real value to the debtor while the latter must pay his debt (166, *cf.* 163).

Law of obligations. — Whoever fails to pay a debt on the date due and has nothing to pay with shall receive an extension of time, but if he still does not pay after the expiration of the extension he must work out his debt (*Ibid.*, 175, *cf.* 167). In all suits, besides the payment of the amount of the suit or Koon, the guilty party must pay damages and costs (179).

Kirghiz law also contains a number of provisions concerning compensation for damages. The expenses and losses must be paid by the guilty person (179), "for the speechless animal no fine or punishment is inflicted" (187). Anyone breaking a Yurt or other building was obliged to pay for the damage caused and also a fine — a horse and a gown (169). If anyone's cattle trample the fields of

another or if anyone mows the grass on another's land, he must pay one half of the damage caused, besides which the mown grass is to be taken from him (170). If a dog which has never attacked anyone before bites a man or tears his clothing it is given to the victim, but if the dog has caused damage thrice previously, the master must give it up and also answer for the damage done (185).

If a suit is decided against a defendant and he dies before settling with the plaintiff, then his son and his brother living together with him are responsible for his debt, as is also anyone else connected with him in his affairs. Those who do not participate in his affairs and whose property is divided from his do not pay anything (177). A guarantor is answerable for the payment of a debt, and if he is poor he must work off the debt for the plaintiff (178). If two or three men, pooling their capital, send anyone to trade in another place and thieves take his merchandise away from him and he takes an oath on it, then he is not responsible (183). Anyone squandering merchandise entrusted to him must answer for it at the end of the set term, and if he does not pay he may be detained for service (184).

Family Law. — Marriage. Marriage is performed among the Kirghiz after the payment of Kalim for the bride. The usual Kalim consists of 32 horses, 1 camel, and 2 servants (118). Polygamy exists. The power of the head of the family, the husband and father, is great. If a betrothed son or daughter enter into marriage with another without the knowledge of their parents, they are put to death. If a son or daughter is not betrothed, then he or she may marry at will, the respective fathers agreeing on the Kalim. But for wilfulness a son pays 9 different horses and 1 better horse (200). The childless widow of a dead Kirghiz goes to his elder brother, and if there are several such widows each brother takes one, but with the consent of their wives and without violence. If a widow refuses to become the wife of her husband's older brother and chooses one of his younger brothers, then the latter must pay the elder 9 small and large cattle. If a widow does not wish to marry again she must not be forced. If the widow wishes to marry an outside person this is permitted, but the property and cattle go to the kinsmen of the dead husband, and the new husband, in accordance with custom, must pay the brothers of the first husband 26 heads of cattle (202)

If a son or daughter renounce their parents and deny that they begot them, then their father may drive them from the house, de-

prive them of their relationship and property, and never receive them again (201).

Minor children who have lost their parents become the wards of the nearest relative, and in the absence of relatives of an outside person of good repute (204). In the same way insane sons and daughters after the death of the father are entrusted to relatives, and in the absence of these they are taken under the protection of the community (205).

Inheritance. — If a son who has separated himself from his father's household should die childless, his estate goes to his father and his wife to his elder brother, and if he has no brother then to his half-brother, and if there is no such one to his cousin, if he has no cousin — to his grandson, etc. If he has no father then the estate goes to his uncle, if no uncle — to his grandfather and distant relatives. If the latter also do not exist then "the estate is divided by the district for the memorial service and feast among the Mullahs and neighbours of the male sex, but to the female sex nothing is assigned" (203). The father and mother could assign to outsiders (in the nature of a memorial) only one eighth part of their capital, while seven eighths had to be handed down as a legacy to the children (206). Wills were made verbally in the presence of Mullahs and relatives. A father or mother could leave one of their sons a share greater than that of the others, and the others had no right to protest (207).

Criminal Law.

System of punishments. — The following penalties are met with in the Customs of the Kirghiz.

Death together with near relatives — C. of Kir., 67.
Death — C. of Kir., 79, 84, 200.
Severing of a limb *(taillon)* — 69, 97.
Freezing in water — 113.
Whipping — 105, 110.
Flogging with rods — 105.
Degrading punishments — 74, 104.
Deprivation of property — 8.
Property fines: Koon, half-Koon, nines of cattle, a horse, etc. — 100, 136, 147.
Fines with people — 116, 68.

Banishment from the community — 114.

Compulsory service in payment of fine or debt — 170, 175.

The Koon was a property fine consisting of 100 horses, 2 servants, 2 camels, and 2 suits of armour.[7] Responsibility sometimes extended also to the district (community) of the offender. The above-mentioned penalties were imposed for the following crimes.

Crimes Against the Rules of Religion. The apostate and blasphemers were to be stoned and if they were not killed they were to be expelled from the community (Art. I). Whoever has heard the blasphemy and did not inform anybody must be punished by a fine — 27 heads of cattle; if he cannot pay this fine, he must be hanged (3). Conversion to Christianity is punished by deprevation of property, and the clear intention of being baptised — by deprivation of life (8).

Crimes against morals. — Anyone raping a betrothed maiden had to pay the bridegroom 1 maid, 1 servant, 1 suit of armour, 1 camel and 24 heads of cattle; and if he failed to do this he was liable to the death penalty (116). For the rape of an unbetrothed maid the offender had to pay the father a half-Koon, and if the maid consented to marry him, also to pay Kalim (118). Anyone raping a married woman was punished by death or, if the husband consented, by the payment of half-Koon. (119). In cases of adultery with the wife of another, the woman's "husband must receive a maid from the offender and has the right to divorce his wife without paying Kalim. If he does not wish to do this, the offender is subjected to corporal punishment" (121). Adultery between close relatives was usually punished by the members of the family without the interference of outsiders (122). If a bachelor committed fornication without violence with a maid and she bore a child, he was forced to marry her and pay Kalim or be put to death (123).

Crimes against the person. — Murder. For the killing of a Hodja the murderer and his whole district (volost) paid a fine as for the killing of seven ordinary persons, and if the fine was not paid then the murderer and 6 of his closest relatives were to be hanged (Art. 67). If a Hodja slew a Sultan or any of the Sultan's kinsmen he paid the same fine, and if he threw out the body and it was eaten by birds and beasts he was forced to pay a one and a half-fold fine of

---

7 In cases of murder where the body of the victim was left in a field the fine was supplemented by 1 camel covered with a rug for the body and 1 maid on a black horse who led the camel and delivered the body of the victim to his relatives.

cattle and one camel covered with a rug for the return of the body as well as one maid on a black horse to deliver the body back to the relatives of the victim (68). If any man fatally wounded another before the judges or killed him, he paid a full Koon, as well as 9 different cattle and a camel to the judge for the offense to them (23). If one or several persons killed one or several others and the relatives of the victim so demanded, they were forced to deliver up one of their number for unavoidable execution and Koon was not collected. If two men killed two others or three killed three, they were put to death or made to pay Koon (84). Anyone killing in self-defence or by accident paid half Koon (85). If a wife killed her husband and was pregnant, she was not punished but was considered dishonoured: if she was not pregnant her relatives could take her back upon payment of half Koon — otherwise she was put to death or pardoned at the will of the relatives of the slain husband (86, 98). If a husband killed his wife, he paid her relatives half Koon (86). Parents were not liable to any penalty for the killing of their children, but if a woman killed her infant begotten in adultery she was put to death (87). For attempted murder wounding, the offender paid half Koon or the best virgin from among his kin (90). For concealing a murderer or aiding his escape the fine was a Koon (91). If anyone died of wounds, the offender paid full Koon for a man and half Koon for a woman, besides the medical expenses (77). A master killing his servant was not punished. If a servant killed his master, Koon was not collected because of his poverty, but if the dead man's relatives so demanded the murderer was hanged (79). If anyone killed a brother or sister living with the family he was severely punished by his father and relatives but not to death; if the victim lived separately the murderer had to pay half Koon in favour of the wife and children of the victim (96). There was no punishment for the killing of a thief, robber or murderer (95). Anyone poisoning another paid full Koon or was put to death (88).

Wounds and mayhem. If anyone wound another or hew off his arm or leg, or inflict any other serious injury upon him, let the same be done to him or let him be forced to pay half-Koon (97). If anyone trample another with his horse, or without the intention of causing him harm, and does him injury (breaks his leg, arm or ribs) he must pay for medicine and be fined a horse; if the injured man dies, he must pay full Koon (100), but if the thing happened purely accidentally (e.g. if the horse bolted) then he must pay only that same horse (103).

Insults by word and deed. If anyone insult a Hodja or Sultan by words or raise a hand to strike him, he is to be fined 9 different cattle; if he strikes him the fine is 26 heads of cattle or his finger is to be chopped off (69). For an insult or blow given by a Sultan or Hodja to a commoner there is no penalty; but if the insult be public and undeserved the fine is 1 horse and 1 gown (70). If a Sultan or Hodja verbally insult or strike another Sultan or Hodja, the offender must apologize (71). Verbal insults among commoners are not considered important and the offender must ask pardon (73) and the same applies to blows; but if the blow be such as to leave a mark on the face, the striker must receive a similar blow and pay a horse and a gown (75). For verbal insult to a woman the offender must apologize, but if the father of a maid or husband of a wife refuses to forgive him the offender must pay a horse and a gown for dishonour; if he refuses to do this he is subjected to degrading punishment by being led round his Yurt thrice with rags of old felt hung round his neck (74). For insults and blows which left no mark given to a woman the offender must beg pardon, for a blow leaving a mark given in a Yurt or on the way he must pay a fine of 8 different cattle and 1 camel (76). Cursing an absent person is not punished (78). For cursing his father or mother or striking them a son is subjected to degrading punishment: he is mounted on a black cow with his face to its tail, old felt is hung round his neck, and he is led around the Aouls and beaten with whips; while a daughter is bound and delivered to her mother (104).

If anyone take away the wife of another without her consent he is to be punished with death; and if with her consent, he must pay Kalim and his best virgin (127); for taking away a servant, the servant's price in cattle must be paid (128); if anyone capture and sell a stranger he must pay his victim 1½ Koon (130).

Crimes against property. — Brigandage and robbery. For taking away a thing the offender must pay the same or a similar thing and 9 heads of cattle (131). Articles taken in armed robbery must be returned together with 1 horse and 1 gown; and if the robber beat or wounded his victim the latter has the right to inflict the same injury upon him or demand 9 heads of cattle (132). Whoever breaks into a house at night and commits robbery is to be fined 27 heads of cattle for a large robbery and 9 heads for a small one; if there is no robbery the fine is 1 horse and 1 gown. If during the robbery he kills anyone, he must pay 1½ Koon; if he kills a man along the way and leaves his body in the steppe, he must pay 2½ Koon (133).

For first theft, the offender must, besides returning the things stolen, pay a fine of 9 heads of cattle for a small theft (up to 1 horse), and for a large theft — 27 heads of cattle with 1 or more horses (up to 7) according to the number of thieves (135). For second theft the fine is ½ Koon, for third theft — full Koon or death (137). For close persons (i.e. Kirghiz from the same community), however, the fine is three times what is stolen (139). Anyone stealing as a result of hunger or poverty must replace what is stolen or give his children into service and himself also go into service (140). If anyone perform Barantu of cattle or horses upon an innocent man must pay full Barantu. If anyone perform Barantu for compensation and drive off more than is due, the surplus must be returned (142,143). If anyone steal anything from a fire, he must pay three things for each one stolen, 9 different horses for each horse, 9 heads of horned cattle for each one stolen, and three sheep for each sheep (149). If a son or daughter steal anything from their father or mother, then the son must be punished by the father and the daughter by the mother without mercy (150). If a wife steals from her husband he must punish her, and after the fourth time he can drive her from his house to her parents (151).

Deception and swindling. Anyone practising deception for personal gain is flogged with whips until marks appear on his body (158). Anyone selling a fake thing as genuine must pay a genuine thing and be expelled from society (159).

Arson. Accidental and unpremeditated arson is not punished. For premeditated arson the culprit must pay the loss, and if a man perish in the fire the offender must pay Koon. If he has not sufficient wherewith to pay the loss and his district does not pay — he is put to death (126).

Organization of Courts and Procedure.

Before the Statute (Regulations) concerning the administration of the Kirghiz (promulgated in 1822), the court usually consisted of one esteemed Bey of advanced age who summoned to his aid anywhere up to 6 Kirghiz of good repute. No second instance existed. But if a case was decided wrongly or unfairly (this had to be proved), then another Bey could be called upon to give a decision (18,31). If the case was decided justly but the litigants brought up new evidence, the case was brought before the same Bey for reconsideration (19).

Fairly detailed rules of procedure existed among the Kirghiz. The evidence of witnesses, oaths, and the results of tracking in case of theft, were accepted as proofs. In a complaint filed by a man, no less than four witnesses were required, in a complaint by a woman — not less than two witnesses (59). The testimony of three witnesses of the best behaviour was required to prove guilt in the deed (43). Women were not admitted as witnesses and could not participate in litigations (48). Cases were decided either on the testimony of person of good repute or on the submission of other clear proofs, e.g. the oath of one of the parties, clansmen or outside persons (61-62). The oath of one man was admitted as proof in cases involving from 1 rouble to 500 roubles. In cases involving more than 500 roubles the testimony on oath of two persons was required (60).

Sources of Kirghiz Law.

Custom. — The basic source of Kirghiz law was represented by their steppe customs. The codes of Kirghiz law, both those which they compiled for themselves (e.g. the so-called "Laws of Khan Tevka" in the XVII-th century) and those which they submitted to the Russian authorities after the conquest (like the "Customs of the Kirghiz," of 1824) had for their base the customary law of the Kirghiz tribes. At the foundation of their social relations lay the patriarchal clan order, and the administration and judiciary were built up on clan principles. Relationship was traced through the father. All these are institutions of customary law. Marriage was exogamous and based on the payment of ransom for the bride, polygamy was allowed, the family was patriarchal in character, and the power of the husband and father was very great, extending to the power of life and death over the children. These institutions likewise are characteristic of customary law. Similarly, the absence of the right of immovable property, the common use of the land by clan unions, and the weak development of civil legal life, are all features of this type. The customs of the Kirghiz were also reflected in the system of punishments, e.g. execution by trampling by horse, freezing in water, whipping, degrading punishments, and finally the property fine in cattle (Koon), compulsory service, etc. This general picture is futher supplemented by such institutions as the responsibility of Aouls and families for their members, the absence of punishments for parents killing their children, for the killing of a husband by his pregnant wife, and for the killing of a servant by his master, etc. The right of the family to judge its members was preserved in the case of incest, the killing of a brother or sister, and theft from the father, mother, or husband. In some cases the practice of delivering a murderer to the relatives of his victim for vengeance was also preserved. Such crimes as the taking away of a servant, the theft and sale of human beings, Barantu (the driving away of another's cattle), trampling by horses, etc. were also clearly customary in character. Thus, custom and customary law lay at the base of Kirghiz law, although they were not the sole source of this law.

Mandatory (Legislative) Provisions. — Among the legal customs of the Kirghiz, a small number of mandatory provisions is also encountered. An example of these may be found in the prescriptions of Khan Tevka, comprising arts. 29-33 of the above-mentioned so-called "Laws of Khan Tevka."

Mongol Law. — The Kirghiz entered into the composition of the Kipchak Ooloos of the Mongols, or the Golden Horde, in which the Yassa of Jenghiz Khan was effective.[8] After the disintegration of the Horde in the XVth century they continued their historical existence independently of the Mongols. Thus they retained the effectiveness of the Great Yassa and the severe ancient law of the Mongols, but did not come under the influence of the later tendency of this law to become milder (XVIth and XVIIth cent.). And indeed, the ancient laws of the Kirghiz (promulgated by Khan Tevka in the XVIIth century on the basis of ancient folk customs) was closest of all to the law of the Great Yassa, as was correctly noted by Professor Leontovich[9]. Thus we often meet here the application of the death penalty which was imposed for murder, robbery, theft, abduction of the wife of another, rape, mixed marriage, and adultery. Parents were not punished for killing their children, etc.[10] Here in some cases the victim could also take the law into his own hands (cf C. of K—95). Of course, it is now impossible to determine the exact extent of the direct

8 The original submission of the Kirghiz to the Mongols was voluntary, but later they rebelled and were conquered and included in the Ooloos of Juchi; *v.* Rashid Ed-din, History of the Mongols, Works of the O. S. Russ. Arch. Soc., XIV, p. 131; XV, p. 115, etc.

9 *v.* "Ancient Mongol-Kalmuck Regulations on Punishments", 1879, p. 245 (in Russian).

10 For more details *v.* Levshin—The Description of Kirghiz-Kaisak Hordes and Steppes, vol. III, pp. 170-178. A French edition (1842) also exists.

influence exercised by the Great Yassa on ancient Kirghiz law. But at the same time it is difficult to imagine that three centuries of subjection to the Mongols, a people of the same nomadic clan-patriarchal culture as themselves, could have failed to affect the law of the Kirghiz. Indeed, the provisions of old Kirghiz law recall those of the ancient law of the Mongols not only in their general (severe) character (as was already pointed out by Leontovich) but also in the case of some separate provisions.

Thus, according to old Kirghiz law (as distinct from laws of other Asiatic nomadic tribes) a husband finding his wife in adultery had the right to kill her on the spot (art. 9). Article 1 of the Great Yassa also provided for the death penalty for adultery, and if we take into account the spirit of ancient Mongol law, such punishment must have been imposed in cases of *flagrant delit* (this being confirmed by Plano Carpini) [11] The old author Pétis de la Croix (in his "Abbregé Chronologique de l'histoire Ottomane", 1768) quotes this fragment in the following version: "Adultery is punished by death. Persons guilty of this crime may be killed on the spot." This immediate killing of an adulterious wife taken in *flagrant delit* was preserved from ancient Mongol law, only in old Kirghiz law. More than this, in the Customs of the Kirghiz of the XIXth century (art. 123) the adultery of a single men with a maid was punished with death (if he refused to marry her).[12] No similar punishment was met with among the other Asiatic nomadic tribes, but the same penalty existed among the ancient Mongols (*v.* Fr. 1 of the Great Yassa;[13] Plano Carpini, *op. cit.*, p. 15).

Death was the punishment for theft of a horse among the ancient Mongols, but it was replaced by payment of a ninefold fine by the thief (*cf.* Fr. 29 of the Great Yassa)[14]. According to ancient Kirghiz law theft was also punished by death or the payment of a fine of thrice nine times the value of the stolen property (*v.* art. 2,

11 Plano-Carpini — History of the Mongols, 1911, p. 15 (Russ. Ed).

12 The punishment for adultery with a married woman had already been changed in the XIXth century. The husband, in such cases, had the right to divorce the guilty wife and to receive a maid from the adulterer without paying Kalim for her. If, however, the husband did not want a divorce, the wife was subjected to corporal punishment (C. of Kir., art. 121).

13 We quote the fragments of the Great Yassa from our book "Fundamental Principles of Mongol Law", 1937, Chap. II, pp. 83-86, *v.* also our "Customary Law of the Mongol Tribes" ,1929, pp. 57-60.

Art 1: "An adulterer is to be put to death without any regard to whether he is married or not".

14 Art 29: "The man in whose possession a stolen horse is found must return it to its owner and add nine horses of the same kind . . . "

17 *cf.*, C. Kir., art. 133), while for a smaller theft, as for instance the theft of a horse, the fine was 9 horses (149, 189); and for theft not exceeding the value of 1 horse the fine was 1 nine of cattle (C. of Kir., 133, 135, 149). Here the characteristic feature is not only the coincidence of the penalty — death, and the alternative payment of ransom, but also the reckoning of that ransom in nines: one or three, in particular for a horse—9 horses.

Let us consider one more example:

As we have seen above, there existed among the Mongols from ancient times the custom of property fines in nines of cattle. We came across this institution already in the Yassa of Jenghiz Khan (*v.* Fr. 29). The punitive systems of Mongol-Oirat Regulations of 1640 and the Khalkha Djirum were based on it.[15] We also meet these institutions among the Kirghiz (*v.* Arts. 23, 28, 69, 131, 135, 141, 147, 149 and 189 of The Customs of the Kirkhiz) — apparently under the influence of the Mongols. Naturally, we may suppose that among the Kirghiz the fine in nines of cattle was also an ancient (and independent) custom, just as it was among the Mongols. But in such a case the custom would have the character of a basic custom in the system of property punishments among the Kirghiz, or at least be on the same standing with the other customs. However, the basic customary unit of property fines amongst the Kirghiz was the "Koon" (100 horses, 2 servants, 2 camels, 2 suits of armour). A Koon or half a Koon was employed as the usual basic punishment; while fines by nines of cattle (or alternatively by units of 27 heads of cattle) were met with as additional punishment, where the Koon system was employed (*v.* for instance Arts. 23 and 28 of the Customs of the Kirghiz[16] and were applied alone only in the less important cases, when the punishment did not exceed 27 heads of cattle. This gives ground for the belief that the ancient basic institution of property fines among the Kirghiz was the Koon and not the fine by nines of cattle; and the latter method was employed as an additional, supplementary punishment. The subordinate secondary position that fines by nines of cattle assumed among the Kirghiz, forces us to consider that it was not an ancient national institution and was of later origin than the Koon.

15 *Cf.* Riasanovsky — Fundamental Principles of Mongol Law, pp. 223, 104, 120.

16 Art. 23 states: "Whoever wounds another fatally before the judges or kills him must pay full Koon; while to the judge, for disrespect to him, he must pay 9 different animals including one camel." Art. 28: "Whoever kills a judge must pay a full Koon, and besides this........8 different animals and one Kalmuck of the male sex."

This gives ground for supposing that it originated from the times when the Kirghiz formed a part of the Mongol Oolooses in which property fines were imposed in nines of cattle.

The Kirghiz also borrowed from the Mongols the *tamgas* — the signs which were put on the clan property.[17]

Mohammedan Law. — The Semitic peoples of the East usually applied the law of equal retaliation, the *droit de taillon* in regulation of the blood-feud. Thus, in the laws of the Babylonian King Hammurabi we already meet an extremely ancient application of this principle: "If anyone injure the eye of a freeman, it is necessary to injure his (own) eye" (art. 196 of the laws of King Hammurabi)[18] "If anyone break the bone of a freeman, his bone must be broken" (*Ibid.* 197). "If anyone knocks a tooth out of the face of a man who is his equal in rank, then his tooth must be knocked out." (*Ibid.* 200). The same phenomenon is met with in Mosaic law with its basic demand of "eye for eye, tooth for tooth, hand for hand, foot for foot, burning for burning, wound for wound, stripe for stripe."[19] The same system was adopted by Mohammed: "O faithful, retaliation for murder is prescribed for you: a freeman for a freeman, slave for slave, woman for woman."[20] But here only the faithful are held in view. If a Mohammedan slave killed even a free infidel he was not put to death. The Koran provided for ransom for murder and the law of *taillon* in cases of mayhem, and quite often applied the death penalty (which was prescribed, for instance, for apostasy) and maiming punishments. Thus, the hands of thieves were to be chopped off, and the punishment for robbery, depending upon the gravity of the crime, was imprisonment, maiming, hanging, or crucifixion.[21]

As is well known, the Mohammedan religion exerted an influence on the laws of the peoples which professed it. Such influence also existed among the Kirghiz.

In the laws of Khan Tevka we find the following fundamental provision: "For blood, revenge is taken in blood, and for mutilation by similar mutilation" (art. 1). "Anyone hewing off another's arm,

---

17 *v.* Levshin. Description of the Kirghiz-Kaisak Hordes and Steppes, *v.* III, 1832, p. 135.

18 Volkov, "Laws of the Babylonian King Hammubrai", 1914. (in Russ.).

19 *v.* Exodus—21, 22; Deuteronomy—22, 24.

20 The Koran, Sura II, 173.

21 For further details *v.* Roberts, "The Social Laws of the Quoran," p. 79.

leg, ear, etc. must be deprived of the corresponding part of his body" (art. 2). These punishments could be substituted for by ransom: death by the payment of Koon (1,000 sheep); for chopping off a thumb the offender paid 100 sheep; for a little finger — 20 sheep (art. 2). For the killing of a Hodja (descendant of a Mohammedan Saint) the Koon was equal to that for the killing of 7 common persons (art. 3); blasphemers were stoned (art. 13); converts to Christianity were deprived of their estates by their relatives, etc.

In the later Customs of the Kirghiz we also find the influence of these principles.

For the killing of a Hodja the offender's entire district was obliged to pay Koon for 7 men, and if it failed to do so then 7 persons from the district including the murderer himself and six of his relatives were to be hanged (art. 67). If two men killed two others, or three killed three, they were put to death or paid Koon (84). "If anyone premeditatedly wound another or hew off his arm or leg, or inflict any other serious injury upon him, let the same be done to him or he must pay half-Koon" (97). A blasphemer was to be stoned, and if he did not die he was to be expelled from the community (art. 1). For conversion to Christianity the offender lost his property, but if he was exposed before his conversion "with the clear intention of being baptised, he must, in accordance with (evidently the Mohammedan) law, be deprived of his life for sacrilege against his law" (art. 8), etc.

It is necessary to note that, generally speaking, influence of Mohammedan law on the Kirghiz was not so strong and certainly weaker than in the Moslem lands of settled culture. Among the Kirghiz the Koran was not applied in its entirety as a religious-legal system, and only a few of its provisions exercised an influence upon the customary law of this people. In this connection it may be stated that there were no (spiritual) judges or Cadis who tried cases on the basis of the Koran.[22] The judges of the Kirghiz were elder honourable clansmen — Beys, who considered cases on the basis of Kirghiz legal customs, which in some cases assumed a religious colouring.

Russian Law. — The influence of Russian law upon Kirghiz law during the period under consideration (before 1824) was very slight. It may be noted that distances were measured in Russian

22 Generally, there were among the Kirghiz no Mohammedan clergy in the sense of a well-defined group.

Versts (C. of Kir., 39), and that for the murder of a Hodja the Volost (district) of the murderer was answerable. The Volost was a Russian administrative division only recently introduced in the Kirghiz steppe. The influence of Russian law made itself felt: 1. In the sphere of administration; 2. In the removal of certain of the most important crimes from the competence of the Kirghiz courts (e.g. by the Statute of 1822 such crimes included high treason, murder, robbery, Barantu, and flagrant insubordination to the constituted authorities, *v.* Art. 206 of the Statute); 3. The institution of a supervisory instance over the native courts in the Okrug (district) administration, consisting of the chief or Okrug Sultan as president and two Russian and two Kirghiz assessors; and 4. In the (somewhat later) mitigation of punishments, i.e. prohibition of the infliction of the death and maiming penalties. Apart from this the Kirghiz customary law outlined above, retained its effectiveness until the Russian revolution of 1917 and the changes attendant upon it.

Fundamental Features of Kirghiz Law.

The Kirghiz are representatives of clan-patriarchal nomadic culture and their law was permeated with the elements of this culture. The Kirghiz were divided into three main branches or Hordes: the Greater, Medium, and Lesser Hordes, as well as the Bukeiev Horde which split off from the Lesser in 1801.

The Hordes were divided into generations, the generations into clans, and the clans into different "bones" (Suyeks), etc. Thus, the Lesser Horde was split up into three generations — the Alimula, Bayula, and Djeti-Urug or Semirodsky. The generation of Alimula consisted of 6 clans, the generation of Bayula of 12 clans, and the generation of Djeti-Urug of 7 clans. The Medium Horde was divided into 4 generations: the Argun, Naiman, Kipchak, and Uvak-Girei. The generation of Argun consisted of 17 clans, Naiman of 9 clans, Kipchak of 9 clans, and Uvak-Oirei of 3 clans. The Greater Horde had three generations: Usiun, Tulatai, and Sargam, which were also divided into clans and which were later joined by the fourth generation of Kunrat — with 9 clans. Each of the Kirghiz clans was split up into separate divisions or Suyeks, and these latter also often had their sub-divisions.

One of the most vivid expressions of the system of clan organization — the blood-revenge for clansmen, existed among the Kirghiz until the most recent times. Thus, by the laws of Khan Tevka

(XVII-th century), the relatives of a murdered man had the right to take revenge in blood for blood and themselves kill the murderer; but if sentenced by the court the murderer could, with the consent of the relatives of his victim, ransom himself from execution by the payment of Koon (*v.* arts. 1 and 2). Academician Georgi, who travelled among the Kirghiz during the second half of the XVIII-th century indicated that at that time the relatives of a murdered man could kill his murderer unpunished during a period of 2 years. After this time they could only demand ransom.[23] The Customs of the Kirghiz of the XIX-th century also contain references to the blood-feud. Thus, if one or several persons killed one or several others, one of the murderers was handed over to the victims' relatives at their demand for execution (art. 84). The relatives of the murderer helped him to pay both Koon and ransom. According to the Customs of the Kirghiz, if a Hodja was killed. the ransom (7 Koon) was to be paid by the entire Volost, and if this was not done the murderer himself and 6 of his clansmen were hanged (67). A wife who killed her husband could be put to death or pardoned at the will of the relatives of the dead man (86).

Clan relations: Blood-revenge for relatives, clan Barantu (driving away of cattle), exogamous marriage and other similar institutions permeated the social life of the Kirghiz a century ago (*v.* for instance Levshin, *op. cit.*). Although this life underwent some modifications and clan ties disintegrated during the century which has since elapsed, a XX-th century investigator, M. M. Kovalevsky, made the following remarks on this question: "Thus, among the Kirghiz people, however far its different branches may diverge from each other, the clan principle is still in evidence in all its force."[24]

The levirate existed, although in a weakened form. After a man died childless his wife went to his elder brother, and if there were several wives each of the brothers of the deceased received one. If the widow wished to choose another and younger brother this was permitted, but the latter had to pay 9 heads of cattle to the elder brother "to whom by law she belonged." If the widow did not wish to marry at all, this was not forbidden. If she wanted to marry a person outside the family, this too was permitted but she was forced to renounce her legacy from the deceased husband, and

23 M. M. Kovalevsky-Clan Life, I, p. 254 (Russ. Ed.)
24 Kovalevsky, *Op. cit.*, II, p. 254; *Ibid.* p. 256.

her new husband had to pay the brothers of the deceased 26 heads of cattle (C. of Kir., 202).

Socially the Kirghiz were divided into two classes: the White Bone (including Khans, Sultans, and also Hodjas — descendants of the Saints of the Moslem calendar); and the Black Bone, which comprised the remainder of the population (including the slaves — former prisoners of war).

The chief occupation of the Kirghiz was nomadic cattle-breeding, with hunting as a subsidiary occupation. The following kinds of cattle were chiefly raised: sheep, horses. camels, horned cattle, and goats.

The right of private property in immovables did not exist among the Kirghiz. The land was placed at the disposal of clan units for use for the purposes of cattle-breeding and hunting. Agriculture was generally little developed, and was practised chiefly in the Greater Horde in the vicinity of Turkestan. In this section it was accompanied by an interesting system of irrigation. The possessors of several ploughlands united to dig a common main canal from neighbouring rivers or lakes, and from this canal distributary ditches took the water to the fields of each participant to the system through pipes. The first of them flooded his field with water, then destroyed the barriers dividing his land from that of his neighbour and let the water go there, the second men did the same with reference to the third field, etc.[25]

Civil legal life was little developed and civil transaction were not numerous.

Marriage was exogamous. In ancient times it was not permitted to take a wife from within one's own clan. Later this provision was modified to the prohibition of marriages within Suyeks and within 6 generations of relationship.[26] Polygamy was permitted but was widespread only among the well-to-do layers of the population. The eldest or chief wife was considered the mistress of the household. It is necessary to note that the Kalim paid by the bridegroom grew with each marriage: more was paid for the second wife than for the first; for the third than for the second, etc. Marriage were arranged by parents and the consent of the children was not required. Betrothal agreements were quite often concluded while the

25 Levshin, *Op. cit.*, III, p. 202.
26 Kovalevsky, II, p. 252.

children were newly born or very young. All betrothals were concluded with the participation of a Mullah. The bridegroom's family paid the agreed Kalim, while the bride's family was obliged to give her a dowry which had in all cases to include a Kibitka for the newly-weds. The wedding ceremony took place with the participation of a Mullah. After this the bride was dressed in the attire of a married woman and the bridegroom subsequently appeared but was long not admitted. He then burst in by force, carried out the bride, and took her to his home on a horse.[27]

The power of the lord of the household—the husband and father—in the family was very great, but in relation to the children the power of the mother was mentioned together with that of the father.

If a husband killed his wife he paid her relatives half Koon (Tevka, 4; C. of Kir., 86), the punishment fixed for the killing of a woman generally (Tevka, 2; C. of Kir., 77). If a wife killed her husband, she was to be put to death and not even the payment of Koon could save her; she could be spared only at the intercession of the husband's relatives or if she was pregnant (Tevka, 2; C. of Kir., 76). The same regulation was contained in art. 86 of the Customs of the Kirghiz, but with some mitigation. Here it was stated that the relatives of the wife were *not obliged* to pay ransom for her: "If a wife kills her husband then her relatives are not obliged to pay Koon, and the murderess at the discretion of the relatives of the victim, is either put to death or, if they forgive her, pardoned." Art. 98 of the Customs of the Kirghiz stated that if her relatives, in pity for her, paid half Koon, they could take her back and the murderess was spared from great punishment. The chief wife could leave her husband if she had good reason to do so, but the other wives could not do this (Levshin).

According to the 5th art. of the laws of Khan Tevka and art. 87 of the Customs of the Kirghiz, parents were not punished for killing their children. But a woman killing her child born of adultery was put to death. If a son or daughter betrothed by their parents entered into marriage with another without their parents' consent they were put to death (C. of Kir., 200). If a son or daughter renounced their parents, stating that they were not begotten by them, the father drove such children out of his house without property and disowned them forever, and the judges could not force

27 Levshin, *Op. cit.*, III, pp. 98-104.

him to take them back (201). Such severe expression of the parental power extending to the power of life and death over the children—had already ceased to exist among the other contemporary nomadic tribes (Mongols, Buriats, Kalmucks, Tunguses, Yakuts and others). A son insulting (or striking) his father or mother in public was mounted on a black cow with his face to its tail and rags of old felt around his neck, whereafter the cow was led around the Aouls and its rider was cruelly beaten with whips. For the same crime a daughter was bound and handed over to her mother for punishment (C. of Kir., 104).

The heirs of a Kirghiz were his sons (and the wife-mother with them), and in the absence of these—collateral relatives. But if a son who had separated himself from his father's household died childless, the heir was his father (C. of Kir., 202, 203). Wills (verbal) were provided for and were to be made in the presence of relatives. The contents of the will regulated the division of the testator's property among the legal heirs (*Ibid.*, 207).

The criminal law of the Kirghiz is distinguished for its severity which was greater than that met with in the laws of other nomadic tribes. The Kirghiz retained for a longer period their independence and predatory way of life and the harshness of their morals and customs. Among the punishments applied we fairly often meet the death penalty (although considerably more rarely in the XIX-th century than in the XVII-th), the severing of limbs as *taillon,* freezing in water, and whipping; but the basis of the penal system was nevertheless the property fine (in cattle). The basic variety of this fine was the Koon — comprising 100 head of large cattle (the dimensions of this fine point to the large scale of cattle-breeding among the Kirghiz). The responsibility of the family, Aoul and even district (Volost) for their members was in some cases preserved.

A particularly characteristic crime among the Kirghiz was the practice of *Barantu.* (cf Arts 142-143). "This evil", wrote Levshin in 1832,[28] "consists of the incessant driving away of each other's cattle and the internecine brawls resulting therefrom. In former years, so they say, Barantu was carried out only in accordance with the sentence of the judges[29] or elders, and then only when the

28 *v. Op. cit.*, III, pp. 84 seq.
29 *v.* Art. 29 of the "Laws of Khan Tevka."

guilty person decisively refused to satisfy the plaintiff. Now, however, anyone greatly insulted, robbed or discontented gathers a band of horsemen, goes with it to his enemy, attacks his domicile and drives away his flocks. It is self-evident that the other defends his property and calls his neighbours to his aid in an attempt to repel the attackers. If he has no time to do this, he rides with his comrades to the Aoul of the foe and they fall upon it together and drive away all the cattle, making no distinction between the guilty and the innocent. Such vengeance is repeated several times, the number of persons involved grows incessantly, flocks and herds are annihilated, the flames of revenge are fanned, and whole thousands of people groan from this evil which is wilfully begun and ardently pursued."

Of course, this phenomenon did not arise occasionally but was a vestige of the ancient institution of the blood-feud. That the Barantu was widespread among the Kirghiz is a fact. The Russian authorities were compelled to spend much effort to weaken and as far as possible eradicate this feature of Kirghiz customary law. But the Barantu persisted all the more stubbornly when the pacification of the Kirghiz and their neighbours made it the only outlet for the traditional predatory daring characteristic of this people.

The courts were organized badly. In some cases the customs of the Kirghiz of the XIXth. century (as the customs of the ancient Mongols) permit to the victims the taking of the law into their own hands. Thus, they permit to kill the thiefs, robbers and murderers without court procedure (cf. C. of K — 95). In other cases the passing of judgment by relatives was allowed, as well as the handing over of a murderer to the relatives of his victim at whose hands he suffered torture and death, cf. laws of Tevka, 2, C. of K — Art. 84, 96, 122, 197 and others. Formerly, in the times of Khan Tevka, the judges were the Khans of the Hordes or the Aoul elders with the aid of arbitrators for the parties. Later the judicial duties were discharged by the honoured Beys of the clans, usually by one, and the right of appeal did not exist. Only the statute of 1822 instituted a second instance over the court of the Beys (the office of the Okrug).

Such, in brief, were the fundamental institutions of the customary law of the Kirghiz. With certain mitigation they kept their character till the XXth. century.

2. JURISTIC CUSTOMS OF THE OSTYAKS, VOGULS AND SAMOYEDS

The Ostyaks are an Ugro-Finnish tribe which lives in Western Siberia, chiefly in the Tobolsk Province and partly in the Tomsk Province. The Northern Ostyaks (Berezovsky District of the Tobolsk Province) — approximately 2/3 of their total number — lead a nomadic mode of life; the others are settled. The Ostyaks are chiefly occupied in hunting and fishing; the settled part is also engaged in agriculture. Their total number at the beginning of the XXth. century was about 25,000 people.

The Voguls are also an Ugro-Finnish tribe, related to the Ostyaks; their major part lives in the Tobolsk Province and part in the Perm Province (Eastern Europe). The Voguls are divided into nomads and settled people; they are engaged in hunting and fishing. At the beginning of the XXth. century there were approximately 6500 souls.

Linguistic researches (Kastren, Reguli) showed that the Ostyaks and the Voguls are close to the Hungarians.

The Samoyeds are an Ural-Altai tribe, close to the Finns, and they live partly in the Western Siberia — in the north of Tobolsk Province, and partly in Eastern Europe — in the north of the Arhangelsk Province. They are chiefly engaged in nomadic deer-breeding and partly in fishing and hunting. Their number is 2000-3000 persons.

The Voguls are very close to the Ostyaks in type and language, while the Samoyeds differ from the Ostyaks in type and language. The Siberian Ostyaks and Samoyeds, due to the proximity of their settlements and their mutual relations, influenced each other (one tribe is even called Ostyak-Samoyeds).

The juristic customs of the Voguls who live in Western Siberia, of the Ostyaks and the Samoyeds, were collected in 1822-1824, when the Russian Government was preparing the codification of the Customary Law of the Native Tribes of Eastern and Western Siberia. Brief data regarding the juristic customs of the Siberian Voguls, Ostyaks and Samoyeds, collected for the aforesaid codification, were published by Prof. Samokvasov in his "Sbornik Obichnogo Prava Sibirskih Inorodzev" (Collection Of The Customary Law Of The Siberian Natives), 1876, (In Russ), ppg. 13-24. In that work the juristic customs, common to the three aforesaid tribes, were given, with an indication of certain peculiarities of the separate tribes (chiefly of the Samoyeds).

Contents of the Jurstic Customs of the Voguls, Ostyaks and Samoyeds, codified at the beginning of the XIXth. century.

Private Law. We meet no indication concerning the private right of owership over immovables: such right was not known. The right of individual ownership over movables is known. Thus "a vitally wounded animal belongs to the one who wounded it first, and a lightly-wounded animal to the one who kills it subsequently" (Art. 22). Among the Samoyeds, as hereditary property, are mentioned "hunting grounds and fishing rivers" (Art. 18), i.e. the right of appropriation of wounded animals and the fish caught (in determined forest and fishing districts). It is prohibited to take out fish or beasts from the trap of another (22). A person taking the horse or cow of another by mistake is obliged to return it to its owner (23).

Of juristic acts are mentioned the loan and the suretyship (Art. 19). For the non-payment of a debt, when it is possible to pay such debt, the debtor is imprisoned, and if it is impossible to pay the debt, such debt is recovered from the surety; if there is no surety — from the debtor in parts, and in case of the debtor's death from his heirs (19). Damage caused to cattle, poultry, damage from fire, loss or damage of things, must be compensated, but if the thing was taken on loan and was lost accidentally, only half its value is repaid or the claim is totally uncompensated (24).

Family relations are built on patriarchal basis, with some weakening of the parental authority in respect to grown children. Minor daughters are given in marriage by the father or grandfather, daughters who are of age may marry an equal even without the consent of the father, but in case of marriage to an unequal the parents have the right to annul the marriage (Art. 17). In case of marriage the bridegroom pays a kalim to the father for the bride (100, 200 or more Roubles), and the wife brings a dowery by arrangement. In case of secret abduction of the bride, the kalim is paid in an increased amount (17). Until the kalim is paid the groom sometimes works for the father-in-law for several years. A step-son can marry his step-mother and sisters, except sisters-germans. Marriage bonds are not strong. In case of controversies between husband and wife two mediators are invited for the purpose of reconciliation; if such reconciliation is not reached the husband and wife are given 4 months, and if no reconciliation takes place within that period the husband frees the wife with half her dowery — first for a period of 3 months (and if she is pregnant — until the birth of the infant and for the period she feeds the child). If after that they reconcile, they may again live together. Such temporary divorce is allowed twice — not more. If the divorce takes place the husband sends the wife and her dowery to her father, and the father-in-law returns the kalim, but such divorce must be deliberated upon by the native Princes or the Elders. In case there are children such divorce is prohibited *(ibid).*

For disrespect the parents and elder relatives had the right to punish their minor children, while children who were of age were punished through the Authorities (Art. 3).

Hereditary norms, as presented in the aforesaid materials, are not distinguished by sufficient accuracy and are brought down to the following:

From the property of the deceased are first of all covered the funeral expenses, then the debts are paid, the will is executed if there is a will, and the balance is divided (Art. 18). It is evident that the will contained no general indications as to the distribution of the property and merely stipulated separate legacies. The children are the heirs, and the sons receive twice as much as the daughters. If there are no sons the daughter receives half the inheritance, if there more than 2 daughter — 2/3 of the inheritance. The mother receives 1/3, the father 2/3; the following is not clear: if there are no daughters, or if there are daughters, or from the share remaining after the daughter. If brothers survive the deceased the mother receives 1/6. After the death of a childless wife the husband receives half the inheritance, the other half goes to her relatives; but if there are children, the husband receives 1/4, after the debts are paid; the wife inherits after the husband in a similar manner. The brothers and sisters each receive 1/6, but if there are more than two brothers or sisters, 1/3 is shared equally; if the deceased was childless and one sister survives she receives the entire inheritance, but if there are many brothers and sisters, a brother receives twice as much as a sister (Art. 18). Apparently, in the first case the brothers and sister receive the inheritance even in case there are children.

Among the Samoyeds the inheritance passes to the children (chiefly to the sons); if there are no children, to the brothers, and if there are no brothers to the distant relatives. If a wife and minor children survive the deceased, the brother must take care of them. A will is allowed by means of granting something to the sons in the presence of the Head of the Clan or Elder; the partition of the property during life is also allowed (Art. 18).

The heirs are responsible for the debts of the deceased.

Criminal Law. The system of punishments among the Voguls, Ostyaks and Samoyeds bore the following character:—

Death penalty — for premeditated murder or poisoning (Art. 13), for unrepented infringement of religious rules and customs and for apostasy among the Mohammedans (Art. 12), for murder in the course of a robbery (when property is taken — the hands and feet are cut off, and death; when no property is taken — death) (Art. 15). The deprivation of limbs — for a theft involving more than 7 zolotniks of silver and for robbery of 7 zolotniks and over (Art. 15).

Punishment by canes — For robbery involving less than 7 zolotniks (Art. 15), for theft among the pagans (15). Punishment with the lash — for the less important religious infringements among the Mohammedans (12).

Punishment by rods — for a harmless lie (16), for disobedience of elders, authorities, clergy (14), for quarrels and fights (20), for a repeated taking of fish or beasts from the trap of another (22), for fraud among the Samoyeds (16).

Imprisonment— for fraud in matters concerning money or things (swindling) (16), for the non-payment of a debt when it is possible to pay it (19), for the violation of religious rules for the first time (12).

Property fine — for an insult to an equal (14), for a non-premeditated murder (24).

Penitence on the knees: for the infringement of religious rites among the pagans (12).

Public reprimand — an additional punishment for fraud among the Samoyeds (16).

Crimes against the rules of religion — for the infringement of religious teachings or rites and for apostasy the offender is held under guard for 3 days; the offender is admonished and if he repents he is forgiven, but if he does not improve then, according to the Mohammedan law, he is punished by death, and for a less important offense — flogged; among the pagans for dishonouring a bear's head, skin or bones, the offender has to make penitance on his knees; for theft from a temple — corporal punishment (Art. 12).

Crimes against a person — Murder. For premeditated murder or poisoning the punishment is death (Art. 13). For non-premeditated murder — a big fine: 100 camels or 700 zolotniks of gold or 7000 of silver (Art. 24). For murder in the course of a robbery — death, and for robbery and murder, as for two crimes — the severance of the arms and legs and death (15).

Insult, offences and disobedience — Offences and disobedience in regard to elders, authorities and clergy are punished by flogging up to 3 and more times, while incorrigible offenders are handed over to the Russian authorities; a person insulting an equal must beg forgiveness and pay a property fine: a deer, clothing (14). For a lie without harm the punishment is flogging (16). For quarrels and fights the offender bears corporal punishment and pays a property fine: an animal or some other thing (20).

Property crimes — Robbery and theft. Those guilty of robbery for an amount of 7 zolotniks of silver are punished by the severance of a leg and an arm; an offender for a lesser sum is punished by beating with sticks. Offenders in the theft of a sum exceeding 7 zolotniks have their limbs severed and are imprisoned and for a smaller theft only imprisoned (Art. 15).[30] Among the pagans theft was punished by flogging and beating with canes and sticks and for a smaller theft only by the recovery of the stolen property (15).

Fraud — swindling. For the fraudulent taking of money or things the rule was that the same had to be taken back or their value paid; if it is impossible to recover such property, or if such property is no longer possessed and it is impossible to pay for it — the offender is held under guard and a yearly payment in installments is made, in accordance with the income of the offender (Art. 16). Among the Samoyeds, however, for the aforesaid crime corporal punishment was the rule and the recovery of the property obtained by fraud plus a public reprimand *(ibid)*.

The organization of the Courts and Court procedure. The smaller cases: quarrels, fights, drunkenness, disrespect, were decided by the nearest elders alone, while cases concerning the partition of

30 Apparently, the severe punishments by mayhem for theft as well as robbery applied only to the Moslems (v. further).

property, matrimonial controversies by the elders with the participation of the best people (6). When there were no such best people the elder reported the degree of punishment to the native Prince or the Commissar, regarding crimes for which corporal punishment was due (Art. 8). In case it was impossible to punish the offender, the case was submitted to the native Prince or the Commissar (2). The more important criminal cases were excluded from the jurisdiction of the local Court and came under the jurisdiction of the Russian Court (13).

The following means were used as evidence: witnesses, documents, oath (7), clues were taken into consideration: foot-steps, foot-wear, testimony, confession (10). If there were no other means of evidence or clues, the case was decided by the defendant taking an oath (Art. 11).

The clan Courts among the Voguls, Ostyaks and Samoyeds had only one degree; the Russian Commissar excercised supervisory functions (3,8).

The Sources of the Laws of the Ostyaks, Voguls, and Samoyeds.

Customs. The basic source of the laws of the Ostyaks, Voguls and Samoyeds were their local customs. The clan organization, the patriarchal form of family relations based on the authority of the father and the ascending relatives, the absence of rights over immovables, marriages for kalim and by working for the bride, etc., the organization of the clan Court, clues, oath, etc., all these are customary-law institutions.

Moslem Law. The influence of Moslem law, which punishes blasphemy and apostasy by death, is noticeable in the severe punishment of the Voguls and other Mussulmans for the unrepented violation of religious rules and apostasy (v. Art. 12). We meet an analogous phenomenon among the Kirghiz.[31] The influence of Moslem Law also told in the severe punishments for robbery and theft. According to the Koran the punishment was the severance of the hands,[32] here the limbs (art. 15), while the punishment for theft among the Voguls and other pagans was considerably lighter (v. 15 — to the end).

The severe norms stated above were, apparently, applied only in respect to Voguls and other Mussulmans. Mohammedanism grew stronger at the time of the Golden Horde during the reign of

31 *v. above*, pg. 16.
32 *v.* Roberts — The Social Laws of the Quoran 79, Riasanovsky *op. cit.*, pg. 211.

Khan Urus (1311-1342), and during the XIV and XV centuries spread among the various peoples who formed the Ulus of Djuchi. It also affected a part of the tribes whose laws we examined above. These tribes were the Shamanists and part of them embraced the Islam. It is natural that the norms of Moslem law found application here only in respect to the Moslems and did not affect the pagans — which can be seen from the end of Art. 15.

It is not clear what norms regarding theft were started to be applied with the appearance of, and to, a third group of natives — the Christians.

Art. 12 also mentions only the Natives Moslems and pagans and maintains silence regarding the Christians. However, with the conquest of Western Asia by the Russians in the XVI century, Christianity began to spread there. In particular, at the beginning of the XVIII century all the Voguls of the Pelimsk district were already Christians. It can be deduced from this that the juristic customs of the Voguls, Ostyaks and Samoyeds, codified at the beginning of the XIX century, arose still at the time when those natives were composed of two groups of Moslems and pagans, i.e. not later than the XVI century, and some of them even considerably earlier (v., for example, the end of Art. 17).

Russian Law. The influence of Russian Law on the laws of the Voguls and others during the period under review was not great. Thus we encounter a certain measure of participation of the Russian Commissar in the administration of justice (Arts. 2,8), the reckoning of Kalim in Russian money (Art. 17), the calculation of fines in silver and gold in Russian zolotniks (24), the rule that the body of a killed thief should not be buried until the cause of death is ascertained (12). This influence was further strengthened with the publication of Regulations in 1822 regarding the administration of the native tribes of Siberia. With the bringing of these Regulations into life (1822-1824) the more important criminal cases were excluded from the jurisdiction of the native court and transferred to the Common Court, then the abolishment of mayhem punishments and the improvement of the Court took place. The customs examined here were being collected just at the time of the bringing of the Regulations of 1822 into life. Therefore, we meet here the customs dealing with murder, robbery and some others and punishments by the death penalty, severance of limbs, i.e., the norms of the customary law in force prior to 1822; moreover, we meet here an indication that "crimes which exceed the competence of tribal authorities, are transferred to the Courts of the Russian Government" (13) — which was soon after actually brought into life; such crimes as murder, robbery, a third-time theft were also excluded from the jurisdiction of the local Courts and punishment by death and the severance of limbs were abolished.

Mongol Law. On the customs under consideration are also noticeable traces of the influence of Mongol laws: the Siberian Voguls, Ostyaks and Samoyeds participated in the Empire of Jenghiz Khan, in the Ulus of Djuchi and were for a considerable period under the influence of the Mongol-Tartars — which, in our opinion, influenced certain legal customs of these tribes.

Thus the Voguls and others know marriage by working for the bride, which existed, among the Mongols and was especially developed among the Buriats.[33] We know that the Tunguses borrowed a similar custom from the Buriats.[34] It is possible that the Voguls and others also borrowed it from the Mongols.

The freeedom of sexual relations is known among the Mongols, before and during marriage, and divorce is easily obtained, by mutual consent as well as by the unilateral wish of the husband, while the absence of children is considered sufficient cause and their presence a certain obstacle; the clan Court deliberates upon the soundness of the grounds for divorce and its material consequences.[35]

We find analogous norms in Art. 17 of the customs of the Voguls and others. Here is also contained the general indication that "marriages are observed most weakly", that the wife and her dowery is sent back by the husband to her father (as among the Northern Mongols and Buriats) and the significance of the presence and absence of children in case of divorce as well as the holding of Court on these matters by the Clan Authorities. It is possible that the customs of the Mongols provided a certain amount of influence here.

Among the Voguls a widow has the right to receive ¼ of the husband's property (Art. 18). We meet an analogous norm with minor variations among the Selenguins Buriats[36] and the Yakuts[37].

33 v. Riasanovsky — Fundamental Principles of Mongol Law, 1937, pg. 239.
34 Riasanovsky — Customary Law of the Tunguses, Nankai Social and Economic Quarterly, vol. X, No. 2. pgs. 186-187, v. further, 6.
35 v. Maisky — Modern Mongolia, 1920, pg. 41 (in Russian), Riasanovsky — Fundamental Principles of Mongol Law, ppg. 146, 147.
36 v. Riasanovsky — Customary Law of the Mongol Tribes, 1929, pg. 161.
37 v. Samokvasov, Collection of Customary Law, 1876, pg. 234 (in Russ), XIV-2,3.

It is hard to imagine that the aforesaid different tribes (Ugric, Mongol, Turki) would have worked out this not quite an ordinary norm independently of each other (even if with certain peculiarities). It is simpler to suppose that they borrowed it from a common source. Such source can be the Mongol Law, as all these tribes formed a part of the Mongol Empire and were under the influence of Mongol culture. An indirect confirmation as to the origination of this norm from Mongolia is the circumstance that it is met with only in the ancient Regulations of the Selenga Buriats of the XVIII century and is not known to their neighbours, the Horins, and other Buriat Tribes. The Selenga Buriats only towards the XVII century migrated from Mongolia to Russia, to the banks of the River Selenga and brought with them their anicient customs. The aforesaid norm is found neither among the other Buriats nor in the subsequent records of the Selenguins. Evidently, it was brought from Mongolia, found no application on the new land and was forgotten there.

We have to note that the aforesaid facts are not a direct proof of the Mongolian influence on the laws of the Voguls, Ostyaks and Samoyeds. It is hard even to imagine such proofs at the present time. But they provide a basis for considering the possibility of such influence.

The Basic Characteristics of the Laws of the Ostyaks Voguls, and Samoyeds.

The materials which we have at our disposal are not extensive and we can only make several indications.

The social organization of the Ostyaks, Voguls and Samoyeds is based on the clan principle and is an organization of a clan type. The aforesaid tribes are divided into clans which have the clan elders who rule and hold Court. Here the tribe princes also survived, occupying a more honoured position than ordinary elders (Arts. 1,2 and 8).

The clan of the Voguls and others is agnate; relationship is recognized through the father and inheritance goes to the father's clan. Certain traces of a more ancient organization are preserved — the matriarchate, when relationship was reckoned through the mother and the marriage of the son to the wives or wife of the father — the step-mother — was allowed (v. the end of Art. 17).

There is no right of ownership over immovables. Civil life is developed very weakly and credit transactions are very few in number (exchange, loan).

Marriages were effected for a Kalim, but marriage by working for the bride is also known (17). It is possible to marry the nearest relatives, except the mother and sisters-germans. Marriage bonds are not strong and divorce is easy.

The inter-family relations are built on patriarchal basis, on the power and the authority of the head of the family, modified by a certain measure of recognition of the rights of the mother-wife, the children who are of age and the control of the clan authorities. Thus the father and the elder relatives have the right to the respect and obedience on the part of the junior members of the family, the right to personally punish the minors of the family, and those who are of age through the local authorities (Art. 3). The father and grandfather give in marriage the maidens who are not of age, but a maiden who is of age may marry an equal independently; the parents can annul the marriage if she marries a person who is not her equal (17). In case of separation the husband sends the wife back to her father together with her dowery, but in case there are children he cannot do so, and the causes of divorce are subject to the control of the Prince or the Elders (17).

In the Law of Succession it is necessary to note the participation of the daughters in the inheritance even in case there are sons, although their portion is less, as well as the participation of the brothers and sisters in case there are children, at least daughters. The Will is weakly developed in the form of special legacies to the children.

In the criminal law it is necessary to note the duality of punishments for certain crimes; light punishments for pagans and severe ones for Moslems (crimes against religion, robbery, theft). The aforesaid duality and the increased measure of punishment for the natives — Moslems was created under the influence of the Koran and the Moslem Law.

The organization of the Court is based on the clan principle: jurisdiction belongs to the Clan elders and the respected clan members. From 1822 the more important criminal cases were excluded from the jurisdiction of the local Court.

3. JURISTIC CUSTOMS OF THE ALTAIS AND TELEUTS.

The Altais, (Altai Tartars) or *Altai Kalmucks,* are a people of mixed Turco-Mongol type inhabiting the southern part of the former Tomsk province /Biysk district/. Evidently they are basically a Turki people, subsequently conquered by the Oirats and intermarrying with them. The Altais lived under clan organization and were divided into clan units — Suyeks (36 in all), while the administrative unit was the Töcün (there were 7 Töcün). At the head of each Töcün stood a Zaisan to whom the clan administration was attached. About one third of the Altais were Orthodox Christians while the rest were Shamanists or Burkhinists (a religious sect). According to the census of 1897 the Altais numbered 19,000 souls.

The Teleuts, Telenguts, or *White Kalmucks* are a small tribe of Turki origin with an admixture of Mongol stock. They too lived under clan organization and were divided into Suyeks. In the XVIIth century the Teleuts, numbering over 1,000 persons, voluntarily became Russian subjects. According to the data of Jadrintzev (1880) they numbered about 6000 persons. They are neighbours of the Altais.

At the present time the Altais and Teleuts enter into the composition of the Oirot Autonomous Region of the R. S. F. S. R.

Some of the customs of the Altai Kalmucks are quoted in Professor Samokvasov's "Collection of the Customary Laws of the Siberian Natives", ppg. 1-3. This collection reproduces information given by the natives themselves at the request of the Russian authorities during the first half of the XIXth century for the planned codification of the customary law of the native peoples of Siberia. However, very little material is given on the customary law of the Altai Kalmucks (only 7 articles), and from arts. 1 and 6 it is evident that these provisions referred precisely to the Altai-Kalmucks. The abovementioned materials contain information on religion, wedding and funeral ritual, and the procedure adopted in deciding litigations.

Some supplementary data on the customs of the Altais may be found in Potanin's "Outlines of Northwestern Mongolia", vol. IV, 1883, Chap. I. Information on the customs of Teleuts is given also in an article "A Teleut Wedding" by Efimova in the "Materials on Marriage and Clan-Family Life Among the Peoples of the U. S. S. R.", 1926. Other interesting data are given in the same compilation by Dyrenkova on clan organization and the system of relationship and family life among the Altais and Teleuts (*v.* her article, "The Clan, the Classificatory System of Relationship and Provisions Regulating Marriage Among the Altais and Teleuts.")

Sources of the Law of the Altais and Teleuts.

Custom. — The customs of the Altais and Teleuts comprised the chief source of their law; for instance: the clan organization, the absence of private property in immovables, marital customs, the system of relationship, levirate, etc.

Besides this, Mongol law had some influence on the juridical customs of the Altais and Teleuts, and in later times the influence of Russian law and customs was also felt.

Mongol Law. — The Altais and Teleuts were for a considerable period of time subject to the Western Mongols or Oirats and subsequently lived in close neighbourhood with them. Travellers (e.g. Potanin) who have described the customs of the Altais and Teleuts pointed to the similarity of the latter to those of the Mongols, and to the influence upon them of Oirat customs. At the present time we do not have at our disposal detailed materials pertaining to the customs of these tribes. But from the available information we can come to the conclusion that the influence of Oirat customs upon those of the Altais and Teleuts was undoubtedly present.

Thus, for instance, there existed from of old among the Mongols, besides the division into thousands, hundreds and tens, also the division into forties (Docin) and scores (Horin). This division is referred to in the Mongol-Oirat Regulations of 1640, and the Russians met with it during their conquest of the Buriats in the XVIIth century. It was long retained by the Oirats and, as was pointed out by Academician Vladimirtzov, it passed from them to the Altais and Teleuts.[38] The Altais preserved this division into Töcün (forties) until the most recent times.

Furthermore it is well known that the Mongols do not bury their dead deep in the ground but turn them over to Nature — as by placing the coffin in a field and either not burying it at all or covering it with a thin layer of earth, and also by suspending the bodies of the dead from trees or burning them. The Turki tribes, on the other hand, usually bury their dead. The Altais and Teleuts

38 "Social Organization of the Mongols", pg. 170, note 4. (in Russ.).

disposed of their dead in accordance with the Mongol custom, i.e. they turned them over to Nature. Because of this, the violation of graves was not considered a dire crime either among the Mongols or among the Altais and Teleuts.

Furthermore, marriage among the Mongols fell into three separate stages, having different juristic consequences and divided from each other by considerable periods of time. First came betrothal, which often took place while the bride and groom were still infants; then the final agreement, when they had grown and the Kalim was paid; and finally the marriage itself (the wedding ceremony). Among the Altais and Teleuts also we find precisely the same procedure with respect to marriage: the betrothal (Kuda); the final agreement (Yargashtik); and the marriage (Ton), with each of these stages having the same significance as among the Mongols. Some of their marriage customs and rituals, as described by Potanin and Efimova, bore a resemblance to those of the Western Mongols.[39]

Thus we come to the conclusion that the customs of the Altais and Teleuts were undoubtedly influenced by those of the Mongols, and that possibly such influence was rather considerable.

The influence of *Russian* culture also took place, for instance, the propagation of the Orthodox creed, the use of Russian coins, etc.

Basic Features of the Customary Law of the Altais and Teleuts.

Both the Altais and the Teleuts preserved their clan organization until the most recent times. They had clan elders who played the chief role in the economic and religious aspects of the life of each Suyek. Until very lately the members of Suyeks used the land in common, and in the more distant past the cattle was also common property. Clan mutual aid was practised during cattle plagues and other calamities as well as for the payment of Kalim. Each Suyek had a common clan ancestor, a clan elder, clan deities and clan sacrifices. Each clan was internally exogamous and one could not marry a woman from the Suyek of his father. Thus, the clan was patriarchal, but vestiges of the matriarchate also existed.

---

39 *v.* Potanin, "Outlines of Northwestern Mongolia", 1883, vol. IV; also the compendium, "Materials on Marriage and Clan-Family Life Among the Peoples of the U.S.S.R.", articles by Efimova and Dyrenkova.

Private Law. — The Altais and Teleuts did not know the right of private property in immovables. Immovable property (the land) was held by clan unions — the Suyeks. Civil transactions were weakly developed. Polygamy was permitted but more recently was not actually practised. Marriages took place early: bridegrooms and brides were 12-15 years old. The consent of parents or elder relatives was required before marriage could take place, but the consent of the bride was also essential. The marriage ritual was divided into three separate ceremonies: the betrothal (Kuda), contract (Yargashtik), and marriage (Ton). Some of the marriage customs were closely reminiscent of those practised among the Western Mongols (sacrifices by the bride before the clan fire, etc.). Marriage was accompanied by the payment of Kalim. At the beginning of the XIXth century the Kalim usually consisted of from 100 to 1,000 head of cattle depending upon the property condition of the parties. After a century, on the eve of the World War, the average Kalim consisted of 200 roubles in money, 2 horses, and 5 pails of Araka, while rich tribesmen gave 300 roubles, 3 horses, and a killed mare and sheep. The bride brought a dowry (of household articles). Marriage was exogamous and it was not permitted to marry a woman from the Suyek of one's father. Marriages by elopement without the consent of elders were also not rare.

The marriage ceremony was accompanied by the singing of marriage songs which were sung by the parents and relatives of the parties but not by the maidens present. The bride and groom were led into the Yurt of the bridegroom's parents in which a curtain was stretched between the entrance and the fire. The ends of this curtain were fixed to birch shafts held by two tribesmen. Having stepped over the threshold, the young couple and their retinue stopped on the other side of the curtain. The Alkyshchi (blesser) read the Alkysh (benediction) after which the young couple bowed from the other side of the curtain to the parents of the groom, as did all the others present, and cried out the appropriate words. Then the curtain was removed and they offered sacrifices to the fire (the domestic hearth). Into the fire a whole cup of oil was poured and the flame rose as high as the smoke-hole of the Yurt. Then all present cried "Bash Bashtym." Besides this, the young couple were led around an empty patch of land under the sun.[40]

40 *v.* Potanin, "Outlines of Northwestern Mongolia", vol. IV, 1883, pg. 29.

The system of relationships among the modern Altais and Teleuts and the marriage norms arising out of this system are of some interest.

All brothers, first and second cousins, etc. within their Suyek went under the same name ("Aga" — the elder, or "Karandysh" — the younger) as did sisters (elder and younger), grandparents and their brothers and sisters all of whom had the same designation.

Relatives on the side of the mother were considered as belonging to another Suyek and not as relatives (in the direct sense) at all. Relationship through the mother was only taken into account within three generations.

Cousins who were the children of two sisters who had married into different Suyeks could marry in the first generation among the Altais and the second and third among the Teleuts. The son of a brother could not marry the daughter of a sister, but the daughter of a brother could marry the son of a sister. It was permitted to marry a son to the younger sister of his mother. Two brothers could not marry two sisters, but one man could marry two sisters (though only if he took the elder first).

The levirate still existed, a younger brother marrying the widow of an elder brother. An elder brother, however, could not marry the widow of a younger: she was forbidden to him.

Vestiges of the avunculate also survived.

Thus a special role was played by the brother of the mother or by the maternal uncle in the lives of his nephews. The maternal uncle commonly rode out to find a bride for his nephew or, if an elopement took place, effected the reconciliation between him and the parents of the bride. He also participated in the payment of the Kalim and was obliged to present gifts to his nephews. His children (cousins) had special privileges and, whatever their age, were considered as the uncles and aunts of their cousins — the children of their father's sister. The children of a father's sister were not permitted to even touch with their hands the sons of their mother's brother (if they did so "their hands would tremble"). Marriage to the daughter of a maternal uncle was permitted and was called "accepting a present from the uncle," but girls were not permitted to marry the sons of their maternal uncles at least until the fourth generation.

There was also preserved among the Altais and Teleuts the curious custom of "Barka", a survival of the epoch of the matriarchate.

Thus Potanin reported from observations made in the 1880's that a nephew had the right to demand presents from his maternal uncle, called "Barka". When coming to visit a nephew, the uncle cut off one of his braids and gave him a horse. If he did not give him a horse, the boy's parents could claim it through the Zaisan.[41] Dyrenkova, who investigated the Altais and Teleuts in the 1920's, reported that among them a nephew could demand from his maternal uncle any article he wished and that the latter was obliged to give it to him and only in rare cases could beg the nephew to accept another thing in place of that demanded.[42]

Thus we find among the Altais and Teleuts not only in the XIXth century but also in the XXth the existence, on a par with the domination of the patriarchal clan order, of strong survivals from the matriarchate: the classificatory system of relationship, vestiges of the avunculate, and the levirate.

Criminal Law and Procedure. — The less important crimes and offences among the Altais and Teleuts were considered by the entire community headed by the Zaisans and Shulengas, and the offenders were publicly put to shame and flogged with rods. More important crimes were referred for judgment to the Russian authorities.

4. JURISTIC CUSTOMS OF THE TARTARS OF KUZNETZK DISTRICT OF THE TOMSK PROVINCE.

The Tartars of Kuznetzk district relate to the Altai group of Siberian Tartars. According to the data of Jadrinzev (1880) they numbered about 24000 persons.

In the "Collection of the Customary Law of the Siberian Natives", 1876, by Prof. Samokvasov, the following customs are given on ppg. 5-11, recorded about 1823-1824.

The Customs of the Natives of Kuznetzk District.

1. The tribute-payers of Kuznetzk District, although all of them generally do not have special generations and are simply called

41 "Outlines", IV, pg. 38.
42 *Op. cit.*, pg. 258.

tribute-paying Tartars, by virtue of their habitations in different places they are called Verhtomites, Mrasites, Kondomites, Zachernites and Niztomites. Those of them who live up the rivers Tom, Mras and Kondoma are called Verhtomites, Mrasites, Kondomites and Shorites, and below the town they are called Niztomites and Zachernites, because they are of the town Kuznetzk and live in the midday side beyond the (river) Chernaya.

2. The laws in respect to religion and religious matters among the Christians are the same as among the Russians; but among the non-Christians, who are idol-worshipers in general, religious functions are performed by means of "kamlanie"[43] performed by the abizes or shamans. Some of them worship wooden idols, others a hare or a bear, the paw of which they kiss even when taking oath. As sacrifice to their idols they always offer the best horse of their herds, which, after being designated for such purpose, even if not slaughtered for a year or more, is most carefully protected against loss and is not sold under any circumstances. "Kamlanie" or the offering of sacrifices takes place twice a year: in the autumn and the spring; "Kamlanie" is performed in the following manner: a light hut (wigwam) is constructed at a distance of 100 sajen or more from the ooloos, always under a tree, in which light hut the shamans perform the "kamlanie"; at the termination thereof, a fire of wood is lit nearby and the people sit around it and drink kumiss made of milk, specially prepared for that purpose; later, near the same huts, five or six slim young birches are planted and on them strips of the hides of various animals are hung, and on a big birch a hide of an animal with the head, legs and hoofs is hung. If someone rides by these hanging sacrifices, or goes to hunt or fish he must worship them, recognizing them as deities. When the offering of sacrifices is thus ended, they return to their homes and there again drink "braga" which is also made of milk; then they return to their yurts. The "kamlanie" by an abiz or a shaman, whom in Russian they call the priest, is never performed without a tambourine in his hands, which is struck with the hand or with a brush specially made for that purpose, and the loud shouting of words which are difficult to understand even for a person who knows their language; he also keeps turning around and around until he becomes like a madman. In the same way is "kamlanie" performed when there is a sick man who is to live or die; in such case they are fully confident regarding

43 The summoning of spirits by offering sacrifices.

the words of the abiz; if, however, the prophecy of one abiz does not come true, then another is called, who is more renowned for his prophecies of the future, and the payment each time is in cattle, money or things, from ten to twenty or more roubles.

3. As in respect to incidents which take place among them, such as thefts, fights, and the like, the following laws exist among them: for example, in case of theft, the culprit, in accordance with the consideration and decision of the bashlik and the community, pays double the value (of the stolen thing) and, in addition, is punished by being beaten with rods. In cases of quarrels, even though sometimes complaints are brought to the bashlik, such cases are usually settled by reconciliation. In cases of dishonour caused to a person of the male or female sex, there are no special provisions among them, the exception being in case a maiden is detected of living dishonourably; her father then has no right to demand as much kalim as he likes from the bridegroom, but such maiden being a dishonourable person he can receive only the price provided for by their law, that is seven roubles or the equivalent of that sum in cattle.

4. In their mode of life those tribute-payers who live among the Christians are like them in everything, except the Zachernites, who do not have houses like the Russians, but who, however, live a settled mode of life. Among the other tribute-payers, who dwell along the Kondoma and the Mrasa rivers, only a few have a permanent abode, everything being of a nomadic nature, the yurts being made of birch-bark, and they travel from one place to another twice a year.

5. Their dispositions are inclined to kind-heartedness; there are very few sly or quarrelsome people; moreover, they are so honest that among them the non-fulfillment of some promise is considered as a shame and defamation.

6. Very few keep their dwellings clean and neat, and then only the Christians, while among the non-Christians there is even no such usage.

7. They are more inclined to hunting than to agriculture or cattle-breeding, which are chiefly the occupations of those who live among the peasants; therefore, almost everyone is well versed in the use of a rifle.

8. The clothes of men are: fur coats, nankeen and bakhta gowns; on the fur coats there are trimmings of white and black lambskins, and among the rich — of otter skins; such fur coats are used by the women even in the summer, under which they put on long shirts made of bakhta or buhkara stuff, red bunting and nankeen; on their heads instead of shawls they wear crimson cloth hats with sable bands; in the winter they wear fur coats made of goat and sheep-skins, thinly tanned and dressed; on these fur coats are trimmings placed around and on the hems which are about two vershoks (four inches) wide, and among the best people these are made of kanfa, foulard, satin and other Russian materials, and sometimes of sable.

9. The tribute-payers cannot be considered either handsome or ugly, because in comparison to the Russians they are swarthy of body, and not odious of form. They seem to be strongly built. When riding on horses and handling domestic animals they are brave; also when opposing their kinsmen and in hunting wild animals; however, the pedestrians are weak and meek, especially against strangers who enter the ooloos. They are respectful and obedient towards the authorities.

10. When an infant is born there are no assemblies and feasting. Among the non-Christians, the newly-born is always given a name by the neighbour who first enters the yurt.

11. The marriage ceremony is as follows: the relatives of the bridegroom come to the parents of the bride and bring with them wine made of milk; they regale the parents and seek their consent to give their daughter in marriage, promising to pay a kalim either in cattle or in money, by mutual consent; and when the kalim is paid in full, the bridegroom takes the bride away and he, as well as the bride's father, invite guests to the marriage — not only those who live nearby, but even those who dwell a hundred or more versts away; each of the guests brings wine with him, which, when brought, is used by all the asembled people.

12. If a person dies, his relatives and friends assemble, and also bring wine with them even from distant places, and they regale each other with wine from small wooden cups; even if there is only a little wine in the cup, they try to drink it so that everybody receives a little. They eat in groups of four or more people; boiled meat with soup is served on wooden dishes, being boiled in a portable iron pot in the middle of the yurt. The dead are buried in

the ground without any rites; but after they are thus buried, a fire is lit in two places near-by — not more than six sajens away; then on the fire which is lit first a horse is burnt, which is killed for the sake of the deceased as well as the clothes which he used to wear; and near the second fire another horse is killed and boiled for regaling the relatives who are in attendance; later everything which has been brought by the relatives and friends of the deceased, such as bread, fresh meat, eggs and other things are placed in hay or grass utensils made in the shape of cups into which, when all the food is eaten, is poured a little of what they call "araki" and everybody drinks for the commemoration of the deceased. The horse on which the deceased used to ride is slaughtered on the spot and is left next to the grave, while his saddle and bridle are burnt on the fire; but if they are unable to call him (the spirit of the deceased?), then everything which is fried and boiled is eaten on the spot; and if they do not eat everything, the remainder is given to the poor, in order to commemorate the deceased; then they all return from the grave-side to the house of the deceased where they eat and drink everything which has been prepared. Wives, after the death of their husbands, for a whole year do not leave their yurts to visit anyone.

13. In case a person falls ill among them, they first of all brew home "braga" (beer), made of barley or malt, which is poured into two big birch-bark utensils, each say with a capacity of six vedros (buckets), and then they call a shaman or an abiz, who brings with him a tambourine, which is a round wooden drum with leather stretched on one side; on the outside of the tambourine there are drawn the moon, stars, a horse, bird, man, fish, snake, frog, and inside on an iron rod there are 15 iron rings. The shaman or abiz coming into the yurt performs a "kamlanie" over the sick man as well as over the "braga"; while he is thus engaged in performing "kamlanie", a horse, cow or sheep is brought in and is given away to the shaitan (devil) if though as a ransome; later, at the end of all this, the shaman tells them that the shaitan came during the "kamlanie" and said that a horse, cow or sheep should be given for the sick man, and then, adds the shaman, the sick man will become well; after this, the animal which was tied during the "kamlanie" is slaughtered; the owner gives to the shaman half the meat and hide, and the other half he keeps for himself, while the "braga" is drunk by all those present. During the "kamlanie" the domestic relatives of the sick man, as well as strangers, are present.

14. The women are more inclined to domestic work than to idleness; and all of them, the males and the females, are very fond of wine. They use bread for food, but sow more barley.

15. The tribute-payers hunt sables, foxes (ordinary ones and silver foxes), marmots, polecats, ermines, smurans, chipmunks and hares (the latter in these parts are called ushkans), squirrels, lynx, otters, bears which come to these parts, gluttons, stags, elks and she-goats; but of them all they mostly hunt hares and squirrels; the hunting of "black ears" takes place in the autumn and winter; all small beasts, with the exception of squirrels and hares, are caught by means of traps with a bait, and they run into nooses fastened to trees; squirrels and big beasts, with the exception of wolves and foxes, are shot with rifles, while wolves and foxes are hunted on horses — the wolves are sometimes killed with sticks and the foxes with a knout.

Basic Features and Sources of the Law of the Kuznetzk Tartars.

The above materials regarding the Tartars of the Kuznetzk district are meagre and do not provide a sufficiently full picture of their mode of life and law.

As can be seen from Art. 3, the Kuznetzk Tartars were governed by their clan elders — the bashliks. The signs of the clan mode of life can be seen from the customs of the neighbours bringing their own wine to their neighbour's wedding (*cf.* the end of Art. 11), as among the Buriats.[44] The same custom exists in cases of funerals (12).

Traces of totemism are noticeable, such as the worshiping of the hare and the bear (Art. 2). A part of them are settled, while others are nomads — chiefly the hunters (Arts. 4, 7, 15). By faith they are partly Orthodox Christians and partly heathens-shamanists; an ancient shamanist custom is preserved among the latter — the horse of the deceased is killed at his grave-side (Arts. 2, 12), which custom is also known to the ancient Mongols (*cf.* The Inscription of Abakansk, 4).[45]

Ownership of immovables did not exists here.

Marriages are by ransom — by paying a kalim, while the entire process (as among the Mongols) is divided into three stages: 1)

---

44 *v.* Riasanovsky — "Fundamental Principles of Mongol Law", 1937, ppg. 53-54.
45 *v.* Fundamental Principles of Mongol Law, 1937, ppg. 240, 241.

previous arrangements relative to the marriage and in particular to the amount of the kalim, 2) a gradual payment of the kalim [and the final arrangements in respect to the marriage (wedding)] and, finally, 3) the carrying-off of the bride by the bridegroom, and the marriage feast.

Punishment for theft — paying double the value of the stolen thing and beating with rods. This punishment reminds one of an analogous punishment among the Buriats, for the stealing of cattle, (yal) only there the fine is four times the value of the stolen thing (*v.* Art. 8 of the Ancient Code of 1781, Customs of the Balagans and Idinsk Buriats, V, I).

Important litigations, e.g. in connection with thefts, were considered by the clan elders-bashliks and the entire community; the less important, for instance quarrels, by the bashliks only.

The aforesaid similarity of the customs of the Kuznetzk Tartars and the customs of the Mongol tribes provides the basis for supposing that in the epoch when these Tartars were conquered by the Mongols, the customs of the latter influenced the customs of the former. The traces of this influence could be preserved until the present time, as for example in the marriage customs and several others.

The influence of Russian culture also took place (Orthodox creed, Russian coins (3, 4). But the basic source of the mode of life and law of the Kuznetzk Tartars is local custom.

5. JURISTIC CUSTOMS OF THE BURIATS.

The Buriats. The Buriats are a Mongol tribe. At the time of the conquest of this nation and its territory by the Russians (in the XVII-th century), they inhabited the regions watered by the Lena and Angara rivers and their tributaries as well as the Transbaikal. By the terms of the treaty of Nerchinsk concluded with China in the year 1689, the entire Transbaikal region with all the emigrants from Mongolia who inhabited it was recognized as a Russian possession. In these regions (the Transbaikal and the former province of Irkutsk) the Buriats still live.

The Buriats were divided into three main tribes: the Bulahats and Ehirites, living along the Lena and Angara rivers, and the Horins of the Transbaikal. Besides this, there live in the Transbaikal other migrants from Mongolia, such as the Selenga Buriats, along the banks of the river of that name, and others. The Bulahats and Ekhirites are known as the Northern Buriats; while the Horins, Selenguins and others are designated the Southern Buriats. The chief occupations of the Buriats are cattle-breeding and hunting, and to a certain extent agriculture.

The number of the Buriats at the beginning of the present century was more than 300.000 persons.

The Buriats were divided into clans. Each clan was headed by its clan chief: Zaisan, Shulenga or Zasaul. A group of related clans was headed by Taisha or Chief Taisha with his Office (Hangalov). State supervision was in the hands of the Irkutsk Provincial Administration.

The Regulations Concerning the Administration of Native Peoples, promulgated in 1822, fixed the following rules: Camps of not less than 15 familes formed an Ooloos, with its clan administration composed of an elected Elder (Zaisan, Shulenga) with one or two assistants. Several Oolooses of the same clan were placed under a Clan Executive Bureau, made up of a Headman and two elected assistants. Several related clans made up a Steppe Council (Duma), which replaced the previous Office, headed by the senior clan chief (Chief Taisha) and containing elected representatives — Taishas, Zaisans and Shulengas. The competence of the clan administration was more precisely defined, and the Native Administrative organs were subordinated to the local court, while the Steppe Council was made responsible to the District administration. This organization, with a few changes, existed until the Revolution of 1917. After the Revolution, in the year 1918, the Buriats organized in Chita the Buriat-Mongol National Committee. In 1923 the Northern and Southern Buriats formed the Buriat-Mongol Autonomous Soviet-Socialist Republic, with its capital at Verkhneudinsk (Ulan Ude).

Records of the Buriat Law[46].

The records of Buriat Customary Law may be divided into two main groups: records of the law of the Southern Buriats (Horins and Selengins Buriats) and records of the law of the Northern

46 *v.* Riasanovsky "Fundamental Principles of Mongol Law", 1937, Chap I.

Buriats-(Balagansk Buriats, Idinsk, Tunkinsk and Kudinsk Buriats and Verkholensk Buriats).

The Horins Buriats

The known records of the Hori tribe are as follows:

Heb (Regulations) of the Year of the Ram (1763). This record contained three articles: 1) On Marriage; 2) On Hunting; and 3) On Measures Against Intoxication. A Russian translation of the Mongol MS. is reproduced in the writer's, "Mongol Law, With Special Reference to Customary Law" 1931 (in Russian) (*v.* Appendix-2.)

The Ancient Steppe Code of the Hori Buriats (1781). The Code of 1781 has not been published and has evidently been lost. Some fragments of this Code were, however, quoted by A. R. in his article, "On the Laws of Some Siberian Natives," in the "Siberian Messenger", 1823, No. 1, and reproduced by the present writer in his "Customary Law of the Mongol Tribes", 1929, p. 156 and also in "Mongol Law, with Special Reference to Customary Law" (in Russian), 1931, p. 137. The provisions contained in these fragments (with some changes) were repeated in the succeeding Codes of the Buriats.

Dzakia (1793). The Dzakia bore the character of an administrative decision and was divided into 9 articles, eight of which contained measures against gambling with cards and dice and against intoxication, while the ninth was directed against abuses in the requisitioning of carts. For a Russian translation of the Mongol MS. see *Ibid.*, App., No. 4.

Hipp-Toktogol (1800). It contained 11 articles regulating trade among the Horins and dealt with the payment of debts and the lending of money on interest. For a Russian translation of the Mongol MS. see *Ibid.*, No. 5.

The Steppe Code (Hipp) of the Eleven Horin Clans (1808). This code was otherwise known as the Statute of 1808. It represented an amended version of the Code of 1781 and contained 131 articles on the administrative, private and criminal law. This is a very important record. The MS. was in Mongol (for a Russian translation, see *ibid* No. 6) and was accompanied by an index of the contents of the Code (41 paragraphs).

The Communal Decision of the Eleven Horin Clans (December 18, 1817). This record dealt with the manner of administration of the eleven Horin clans. In its 22 articles it depicted the administrative organization of the Hori Buriats prior to the epoch of the Regulations of 1822 relating to the administration of the native tribes of Siberia. For a Russian translation of the Mongol MS. see *Ibid.* No. 7.

The Decision of the Eleven Horin Clans (May, 1818). It contained six articles on internal administration, on the collection and distribution of taxes and on Courts, etc. Article 4 contained the history of the origin of the three Taishas of the Horin clans and the order of succession to these offices. A Russian translation of the Mongol MS. may be found in *Ibid.* No. 8.

Communal Decision of the Eleven Horin Clans (October 27, 1820). This item was divided into 7 articles or points dealing with the collection of taxes and dues. Mongol manuscript.[47]

Statute of the Hori Buriats (March 30, 1823). It was published in the "Collection of the Customary Laws of the Siberian Natives", by Professor Samokvasov, in 1876.

The record was divided into 12 chapters and 144 articles. The first chapter dealt with temples, the Bourkhans and the Lamas; the second with the way in which diputes were settled which arose between Lamas, officials and commoners; Chapter III with the various lists, the Yassak and other taxes and their payment; Chapter IV with the discharge of official duties; Chapter V with the collection of local dues, rewards, and the upkeep of local and district postal stations, as well as the repairing of roads; Chapter VI. Matchmaking and litigations between husbands and wives; Chapter VII. Debts; Chapter VIII. Control of the consumption of alcoholic liquors and the playing of cards; Chapter IX. Theft and searches; Chapter X. Trespassing on pastures, allotment of hay and corn fields and the purchase and sale of corn; Chapter XI. Precaution against fire, incendiarism in forests, and the supply of carts to Oolooses; Chapter XII. Miscellaneous matters.

The Horin Statute of 1851. The Statute consisted of 197 articles and 19 sections. The contents of the section were as follows: The first eight sections dealt with the clergy and their needs. 9. On the Duties of Officials of the Administration of the Hori Buriats; 10. On the Safeguarding of Fields and Meadows; 11. On Carts Kept for Government and Public Use in the Horin Region; 12. On the Con-

47 *v.* the article by Jamtsarano and Turunov: "Review of Records of the Written Law of the Mongol Tribes", Proceedings of Irkutsk University, I.

struction and Upkeep of Roads and Bridges; 13. On Betrothals and Weddings; 14. On the Decision of Lawsuits; 15. On Measures against Drunkenness, and Cards and Other Gambling Games; 16. On Searches for Stolen Property and Judgment in Such Cases; 17. On Measures Against Fire and Relief to Sufferers from Fire and Flood; 18. Miscellaneous; 19. On Outrages and Slanders.[48]

The Selenguins Buriats.

The Ancient Code of the Selenguins. From the resolution of June 5, 1823 (see below) it is evident that the first Steppe Code was adopted by the Buriats of Selenga (the Selenga river) between 1765 and 1818.[49] And indeed, information has recently come into the possession of the writer, to the effect that the ancient code of the Selenga Buriats (dated 1775) has been found.[50]

The Statute of the Selenga Buriats (*June 5, 1823.*) This record of the customary law of the Buriats of Selenga is contained in the collection compiled by Samokvasov, on ppg. 149-197 of the work.

The record was divided into 9 chapters and 180 articles. The chapters were as follows: I. On the Theft of Cattle, etc.; II. On Discord between Husband and Wife, and On Cattle given as "Kalim"; III. On Verbal Disputes and Fights; IV. On Medical Treatment and the Reading of the (sacred) Books; V. On Debts and Lawsuits; VI. on Inherited Estates; VII. On the Care of Fields and Meadows; VIII. On cattle pastures; IX. On the Election of Elders, etc.

The Selenguin Code of 1818. In the resolution of June 5, 1823, already quoted, mention was made of the fact that in 1818 the Buriats or Selenga assembled for a Seim in accordance with the order (inquiry) of the authorities, and adopted a code similar in content to a former one composed on the basis of certain traditions, i.e. they apparently altered and completed the code already in force. This amended code is not known to us but it does not seem to have differed much from the Statute of 1823 and probably served as the basis for the latter.

---

48 *v.* the already mentioned article of Jamtsarano and Turunov.

49 *v.* Riasanovsky, "Customary Law of the Mongol Tribes", pg. 160.

50 The author has at his disposal some articles of this Code. From their contents one may suppose that the Code of 1775 served as the basis for the Statute of 1823.

Records of Customary Law Common to the Horins and Selenguins.

The following written collections of the Juristic customs common to the Selenga and Hori Buriats contained data relating to the customary law of the Transbaikal Buriats as a whole.

The Tzaadza (Law, Decree, Prohibition) of 1759 was a record purely religious in character. A Russian translation of the Mongol MS. was published in the writer's "Mongol Law, With Special Reference to Customary Law", Appendix—I.

The Conciliatory Regulations (*Hipp-Toktogol*) *of 1788.* These applied both to the Hori and Selenga Buriats, and contained ten articles dealing with the law of marriage. For the Russian translation of the Mongol MS., see *Ibid.*, Appendix—3.

The New Rules (Shine Toktogol) of 1841. This work contained 54 articles divided into three parts as follows: I. On the Lama Priesthood; II. On the Insignia and Uniforms of Chiefs and Honorary or Public Officials; III. On Wedding Banquets; and supplementary articles.[51]

The Buriats of Balagansk.

On April 1, 1818, the 17 clans of the Balagansk Buriats, at a joint meeting, adopted a memorandum for submission to the Russian authorities.

This memorandum comprised six questions with their answers, concerning the courts, private law, criminal law, the rights and duties of the chief Taisha and heads of the clans.

This record has been published in the article by Hangalov "Juridical Customs of the Buriats", Ethnographic Review, 1894, 2, pg. 101 etc.

The Balagansk, Idinsk, Tunkinsk and Kudinsk Buriats.

Information concerning the customs of this section of the Buriats is contained in ppg. 87-105 of Samokvasov's book. The material is divided into eight chapters: I. On Religion; II. Cases Judged

51 *v.* the previously mentioned article by Jamtsarano and Turunov.

by Chiefs of Clans; III. Judicial Procedure; IV. On Regulations Applied by the Natives to Various Crimes; VI. On Marriages and Disputes Concerning the Kalim; VII. On the Extent of the Power of the Native Chiefs; VIII. On the Rights of the Natives.

The Buriats of Verkholensk.

Materials referring to the juristic customs of the Buriats of the District of Verkholensk are given on ppg. 77-85 of Professor Samokvasov's collection. The material is divided into ten chapters as follows: I. The Chiefs and System of Administration (15 articles, comprising provisions relating to procedure and punishment). II. On Native Marriages (13 arts.); III. On Wives Deserting Their Husbands and On Wives and Husbands Who Have Been Baptised (5 arts.); IV. On the Customs of the Steppes (Land Ownership) (7 arts.); V. On the Damage Caused to Fields by Cattle Grazing on Them (4 arts.); VI. On Taxes (3 arts.); VII. On Public Revenues (2 arts.); VIII. Explanations Governing the Customs and Laws of the Steppes (2 arts.); IX. On the Election of Native Chiefs; and X. Supplementary Articles to the Preceding Chapters (6 articles, on the Courts, On Insults and On Marriage.)

We do not give here the contents of the Buriat Law, as we did it in previous works[52]. But we explain here in more detailed form the basic features of Buriat law[53].

Sources of Buriat Law

Custom. Juridical customs comprise the main source of Buriat law.

The customs of hospitality, the principles of mutuality and reciprocal aid, the clan system and co-operation between tribes were characteristic of the life of the Buriats. The patriarchal clan order lay at the base of their social relations. The principles of solidarity and mutual aid were well developed. The administration and judiciary were built up on clan and tribal lines. Relationship was recognized only through the father. The family was patriarchal in character and was based on exogamic marriage, polygamy being permitted, on the ransom of brides and the strong power of the husband and

52 *v.* in detail - Riasanovsky "Customary Law of the Mongol Tribes", 1929, part II, and in particular "Mongol Law", 1931, part II (in Russ.)

53 *v.* further.

father of the family. The use of the land was partly tribal, partly family in character, but the beginnings of individual property in land were also present. Crimes were not complex, the chief of them being personal insult and the theft of cattle. The system of punishments was based on property fines and flogging. Responsibility often spread to the entire family. The entire social organization outlined here stemmed from customary origins.

The customs met with among the Buriats had different origins. Some of them represented customs common to all or most nomadic tribes of clan-patriarchal culture. Such, for instance, was the custom of clan organization, the absence of the right of immovable property and the utilisation of the latter by clan union for purposes of cattle-breeding and hunting, exogamy, polygamy, ransom for brides (Kalim), the reckoning of relationship in the male line, property fines (in cattle), etc. Another group of customs, was common to the Mongol tribes as a whole and stemmed from a common Mongol source, such as the right of sons to an allotment of property, the inheriting by the younger son of the household of the father, property fines in nines of cattle (a survival of which existed in the Buriat "Yal"), the mild attitude towards adultery, flogging with the knout, etc. Some customs respresented phenomena peculiar to the life of the Buriats. Among these were customs connected with the irrigation of haymows (and ploughlands), the renting of land by Buriats to Buriats, exchange marriages (in which the son of one family married the daughter of another, while the daughter of the first family married the son of the second), flogging with rods, etc. Furthermore, among the Buriats themselves we perceive difference of legal customs, a kind of legal particularism. Thus, the legal customs of the Northern Buriats (Bulahats and Ekhirites) were different from those of the Southern Buriats (Horins and Seleguins), this difference being expressed in some provisions concerning compensation for damages and losses caused, the allowed rates of interest, some provisions concerning marriage, etc. Finally, among the Southern Buriats we meet a certain particularism of legal provisions, e.g. between the Horins and Selenguins, and the same phenomenon is evident among the northern Buriats e.g. among the Buriats of Balagansk and Verkholensk.

Russian Law. Old Russian law had certain influence on the Buriat law. The Russian influence in the sphere of criminal law expressed itself among the Buriats through the consideration by the common judicial institutions of important "criminal" cases involving

Buriats and also through the consideration by the district courts of cases coming to them as appeals against the decisions of the tribal courts and police.

Russian private law exercised its influence chiefly in the sphere of property and obligatory relations. Thus it found application in the domain of agriculture. The transition of the Buriats, especially those of the North, to agricultural ways of life which took place under Russian influence, was to a substantial extent accompanied by the growth of rent relations which were formerly unknown among the Buriats (Customs of the Buriats of Verkholensk 38,50) and in separate cases led to the establishment of private ownership in land (Customs of the Selenga Buriats, 163; Customs of the Verkholensk Buriats — 38,40.) This transition was connected with the further evolution of Buriat Law: the enclosure of fields (C. of S. B. 154, 155, 163; C. of H. B. X-8, XII-26; Steppe Code-74, 78), compensation for trampling of crops by cattle (C. of V. B.-41, 44). There were references to the development of rent, etc. The general development of money-economy gave rise to the appearance of percentage loans with a maximum allowed rate of 12 per cent (C. of H. B.-VII, 5; of Sel. B.-103), as it existed in old Russian law and generally such credit transactions as existed among the Russians, and also the Russian institution of the ten years prescription.[54]

The influence of Russian law upon the law of the Buriats became much stronger in the 50 years preceding the Russian Revolution, in connection with the general cultural development of the Buriats. At this time an important channel through which Russian law exercised its influence was the "Code of Steppe Laws of the Nomadic Peoples of Eastern Siberia" which was effective among the Buriats and in which, on a par with the codification of native law, the gaps of the former were filled by provisions of Russian law.[55]

54 Cf. also the maximum term of personal service (5 years) and some others.

55 The influence of Russian customs was noticeable also in other cases. Thus, together with the borrowing of agriculture from the Russians there were also borrowed Russian customs connected with this occupation, e.g. in Art. 74 of the Steppe Code of 1808 of the Buriat Horins (Lamaists) there is mention of punishment for the grazing of cattle on grain fields after the feast of the Intercession of the Holy Virgin (a festival of the Russian Orthodox Church taking place of 1/14 October). Or the plots of land destined for agriculture should be fenced from 9th May to 15th September of each year (C. H. B. - XII, 26, C. Sel. B - 154, 164). 9th May and 14th September (Old Style) are also the feasts of the Russian Orthodox Church. Or, as e.g. in a decision of the Horins (Dec. 18, 1817) it was prescribed that all community archives were to be kept in Russian houses and not Buriat Yourts.

It is, therefore, not surprising that when in 1918, after the Russian Revolution, the Buriats convened their national Buriat court, this court was permitted to use Russian material law in so far as it did not contradict the sense of justice of the Buriat people (*v.* Art. 4, of the Novel No. 3, on the Buriat National Court and 66 of the statute on Judicial Procedure in the Hoshun and Aimak Courts.) This circumstance is sufficient proof of the fact that Russian law had a marked effect on the legal consciousness of the Buriat. However, this influence was not decisive and did not supersede local customs, which remained the fundamental source of Buriat law.

The Buriat law contains also some *mandatory* (legislative) provisions and some provisions under the *lamaist* church influence.

The Basic Features of Buriat Law.

The Buriats are representatives of the nomadic patriarchal clan mode of life.

The Buriats were divided into three main tribes, the Bulahats, Ekhirites and Horins, and into separate "generations". The tribes, in their turn, were divided into clans (about 200 in all) which had from the most ancient times been governed by their clan chiefs—the Shulengas and Zaisans. At the head of each tribe stood a Taisha. The Buriat clans, for the most part, drew their names from the names of the localities and rivers in which the camped. Thus, in the province of Irkutsk, there were 1. the Tunkinsk Buriats—14 clans; 2. Kitoisk—3 clans; 3. Kubinsk—16 clans; 4. Kapsalsk—4 clans; 5. Alarsk—11 clans; 6. Balagansk—24 clans; 7. Idinsk—29 clans; 8. Verkholensk—7 clans; 9. Lenski—7 clans; 10. Olkhonsk—9 clans; 11. Nijneudinsk—2 communities. In the Trans-Baikal region there were the Buriats of 1. Barguzinsk—5 clans; 2. Kudarinsk—4 clans; 3. Selenga—38 clans; 4. Hori—14 clans (11 old and 3 new); 5. Aginsk—10 clans. Besides this, there existed a number of separate generations. These tribal units served as a basis for the former Russian organization of the Buriats.[56] The administration and judiciary, in the lower instances, were represented by the clan chiefs, whose authority, according to Hangalov, who wrote concerning the end of the XIX-th century, was very great.[57] Each tribe,

56 The Buriats also preserved a vestige of the old military organization, the division into Horins (scores). *v.* Bogdanov, "Outlines", pg. 101.

57 *v. Hangalov,* "Juridical Customs of the Buriats", *Ethnographic Review* (Russ.), No. 2, 1894.

and each clan within the tribe, was obliged to camp on the territory allotted to it. The Buriats paid a Yassak (levy, formerly consisting of furs) by clans and through their clan chieftains. Common family property existed (individual property in movables also being permitted), and even common family responsibility. Relationship was recognised in the male line. For insults to parents and senior clansmen increased penalties were imposed.

Private Law. Family relations among the Mongol tribes were based on exogamous marriage. Among the Buriats marriage also bore an exogamous character and relationship in the male line served as a bar to marriage. Remnants of the matriarchate existed among the Buriats as among the other Mongol tribes.

Among the Buriats the mother's clan was called the Nakhsanut, i.e. the clan of the maternal uncle (Nakhsa—maternal uncle). The Buriat himself, in relation to this clan, was called Ze-hu-bun, i.e. nephew through the sister. The entire Nakhsanut clan patronised its Ze-hu-bun and treated him with gentleness and concern, being obliged to help him in difficult times and care for him in misfortune. The Ze-hu-bun, in his turn, manifested respect for all members of the maternal clan as his seniors, even though the younger members of this clan might be young enough to be his grandchildren. He commonly addressed all of them as "Nakhsa" and treated them with respect and courtesy. Marriages with the Nakhsanut clan were considered particularly auspicious. The Buriat was obliged to show a special respect likewise towards the clan of his wife. He was obliged to address all its members, even the youngest, as "Akhe" (senior) and tolerate indifferent treatment from them. A son-in-law was bound to bear everything in silence and could not reply even to reprimands and scoldings administered by his wife's relatives. To scold the father or brothers of one's wife was considered a great sin.[58]

We do not meet with group-marriage among the Mongol tribes but only marriage between a definite man and definite women, i.e. permanent marriage in its polygamous form. Nevertheless some vestiges of the previous epoch (of group marriage) may be noted. For instance the Buriats evidently practised some time ago hospitable haeterism (v. Petri *ib.*, 25).

There existed among the Buriats yet another survival from the group marriage, the levirate. Under the levirate a widow became

58 *v.* Petri-"Marriage Provisions", ppg. 27-29.

the wife of the younger, or one of the other brothers of her deceased husband. This institution is a survival from the community of wives among close relative—brothers.[59] It outlived the epoch of the matriarchate and was met with among peoples which had attained a higher level of development, e.g. the Jews, Greeks and Hindus. The same custom could be observed among the Northern Buriats. In the Customs of the Verkholensk Buriats we may read the following: "A wife taken in exchange, or in default of this for Kalim, has no right whatever to separate herself from her husband, all the more if there are children living with her (art. 20); in the event of the husband's death she has no right whatever to separate herself from his relatives, since in payment for her the husband's sister or other close kinswoman was given, or Kalim; and in this case she is bound to become the wife of her husband's brother, or his other close relative, or even of her father-in-law." (art. 21, *cf.* art. 90 of the Steppe Code.)

But in Buriat law the custom of the levirate was modified and lost its strongly obligatory character. A widow could refuse to marry a brother-in-law or other relative of her husband, in which case a property settlement was made, the parents of the husband being obliged to marry off the widow to another and appropriate the Kalim, which was paid to the husband's heirs. On the other hand, if none of the relatives of the deceased husband wished to take his widow to wife, she was considered free except that, if she married, the Kalim given for her was to go to the heirs of her first spouse (arts. 21, 22).

Mongol law recognized polygamy as a customary institution of family law.

The Buriats, as was pointed out by Georgi in the XVIII-th century, "can take to themselves as many wives as they can buy. Some have four or five, many only two, and the others, whether from poverty, modesty or love, have only one." (*cf.* C. Sel. Bur. 59,60; Verkhol-Bur. 17 suppl).

Among the modern Buriats polygamy exists but is now not widespread. Thus, according to the customs of the Selenguins, if a couple was childless or especially had no sons, the husband could, with the consent of the first wife, marry another, and if there were

59 Some sociologists (Bachofen, MacLennan, Kautsky) see in the levirate a survival from the practice of polyandry (the group marriage of brothers with one wife.)

still no sons, he could take a third wife, with the consent of the first two. It was prohibited to have more than three wives (59). However, even if a Buriat had a son, but needed a second wife, he could marry again with the consent of the Lamas and chief Elders, these giving permission if they found that he had good cause to desire another spouse. Marriage without such permission was punished (60). In the Code of Steppe Laws of 1841 this rule was promulgated for the Buriats of Hori, Selenga and Barguzinsk. The Northern Buriats, according to Hangalov, seldom had two or three wives. The cases where they did were commonly the outcome of the barrenness of the first wife and the failure of the second to bear sons, in which case they were obliged to take a third (Hang., 6). The first wife of a Buriat was considered superior in the household and supervised the domestic economy, the second and third wives being obliged to obey her and being considered as her younger sisters. No Buriat commonly had more than three wives. Most of the Buriats had only one wife, the chief cause for this being the economic position of the majority and the absence of sufficient reasons for a second marriage. Besides this, the spread of Christianity among the Northern Buriats played a large part in this process. Thus it is possible to say that the modern Buriats are close to monogamy.

Vestiges of the form of marriage by abduction are met with in Buriat law. Among the Northern Buriats even at the present time, abduction with the consent of the bride is practised in cases where the bridegroom is unable to pay the Kalim and the bride's parents refuse to give her up. The abduction is carried out with the participation of all the young men of the husband's clan (Petri).

As is known, disputes between tribes and clans resulting from the abduction of brides were in time replaced by payment of a ransom or purchase price by the abductors. A vestige of this practice is payment for brides (the Veno, Kalim, etc.), which gives to marriage an appearance of purchase.

This latter form of marriage was the one recognized by Mongol law as customary and widespread.

Buriat law calls such ransom by the name of Kalim (Steppe Code, 12,13; C. of Hor. B., VI, 1,2, etc.; C. of Verk. B., 17,19; C. of Bal. and other B., VI, Hangalov's "Juridical Customs" 3, etc.), such Kalim having once been paid in cattle but more recently in money.

Buriat law preserved yet another ancient form of marriage—by working for the bride, a form that takes us back to Biblical times and is reminiscent of Jacob's labour for Laban, first seven years for Leah, then seven years for Rachel. In Hangalov's "Juridical Customs" the following more detailed provision is quoted. If anyone, in consequence of poverty, was unable to pay a Kalim and marry, he was hired as a worker on the condition that he works a certain number of years for which his master would pay his Kalim and thus enable him to marry and, after the expiration of the term fixed for his labour, let him go, giving him a horse with harness, plough, harrow, a sledge, a cow with a calf, a mare with a colt, a sheep with a lamb, and goat with a kid. Sometimes the master built him a house or a yurt and gave him a dessiatine of ploughland and a dessiatine of sown land, for which the worker was obliged to labour for from 6 to 8 years (Hang., "Jur. Cust.", 7.). Such a master was usually one of the bride's relatives or even the future father in law. In arts. 347-349 of the Code of Steppe Laws of 1841, mention is likewise made of working for a bride's parents to pay for the bride. B. E. Petri wrote concerning this: "The custom of working for a bride has its origin in hoary antiquity. Young people, having no possibility of paying the Kalim, went to the clans of their affianced brides and lived there as ordinary labourers for a stipulated number of years. . . . Working for the bride is still practised at the present time, with the difference that half the Kalim is now supposed to be paid in money while the other half may be worked for."[60]

Buriat law also takes cognizance of matchmaking and mutual marriage or "Anda" as it is called among the Southern Buriats, or marriage "by exchange" among the Northern Buriats, when two pairs of children of two fathers marry among themselves; for instance the son of the first marries the daughter of the second and *vice versa* (St. C., 14; C. of Hor. B., VI, 1,2, etc.; C. of Verkh. B., 17, 19; C. of Bal. and other B., VI; Code of Steppe Laws, 343, 304). In such cases the Kalim was mutually cancelled this arrangement forming the economic bases for this variety of marriage.

In Buriat law divorce did not present any great difficulties. Divorce was allowed in cases of mutual consent, of the unilateral desire of the husband, and the persistent reluctance of the wife to live with her husband (with different property consequences).

Divorce by mutual consent was perfectly free, the dowry being returned to the wife (C. of Hor. B., VI, 7; C. of Bal. & other B., VI, 2). Divorce by the unilateral desire of the husband (e.g. in the

60 *Op. cit.*, pg. 19.

case of a childless wife) was also allowed (C. of Hor. B., VI, 7), and even as a result of the husband's simple reluctance to live with his wife (C. of Sel. B., 49; C. of Verk. B., 26), but in such cases the Kalim was not returned. Finally, divorce was also permitted at the expressed desire of the wife, e.g. in the case of insistent reluctance (C. of Sel. B., 51,52; C. of Verkh. B., 26, 27,-Petri) but in this case Kalim was returned.

Among the Buriats the paternal power was shared by both parents, although in the lifetime of the father his authority was predominant. No wonder that in the Customs of the Balangansk, Idinsk and other Northern Buriats it was provided that: "a wife taken by a Buriat in marriage is esteemed as one bought but not a serf, being his equal helper in their mutual life". (VI, introd.)

After the death of her husband, the Buriat widow could go on living with her children, in which case she remained the full mistress of the house and could dispose of all the property at her absolute discretion. She brought up her children, married off her sons, paid Kalim for their wives, etc. But a widow could also take her dowry and go back to her parents or relatives, and could marry again if she wished (Hangalov, "Jur. Cust.", 7; C. of Hor. B., 6, 11, 16; C. of Sel. B., 61, 62, 65).

Although the parental power was great, the children were not defenceless.

Under Buriat law, parents were obliged to provide for their children, bring them up, give them dowries, and endow them with property at separation (Horin Code of 1781; C. of Hor. B., XII, 6; C. of Sel. B., 130; Hang. "Jur. Cust.", 1, 2.) Buriat law thus provided not only for the rights of parents with respect to their children, but also for their duties with respect to the later.

Modern investigators of the life of the Mongols and Buriats (such as Maisky and Petri) confirm the fact that although the authority of the husband and father in the family is quite strong, it is not despotic in character; and family relations are permeated with mutual tolerance, the concern of parents for their children, etc.

The origin of private property among the Buriats was connected with personal labour and exploit.

A hunter killing a beast acquired the right of ownership over its carcass and skin; and anyone catching a fish or animal in a net or trap had the right of ownership over the living animal and the caught fish. If the hunt or fishing expedition bore a common character, there arose the right of common ownership which was followed by equal division of the game. According to the customs of the Horins, if anyone wounded a fox or wolf and gave chase to the wounded beast, and if the beast was slain by another hunter, the beast belonged to the first hunter and its four paws to the second. But if the first wounded a she-goat and the second killed it, the entire beast belonged to the second (St. C., 104). It was presumed that for a small beast the first shot was fatal, while for large game the fatal shot was the second. The customs of the Selenguins differed somewhat from those of the Horins. Among them the first hunter who wounded the beast and the second who killed him divided the game evenly. If anyone was a witness of how a hunter killed a sable, fox or wolf, he was entitled to the forepaws, while if a large beast was killed, such as a wild goat, boar etc., the witness received the hindquarters (Code of 1775, 129; C. of Sel. B. 142). During the formerly customary community hunts (Aba) only participants in the hunt were recognised as such witnesses, i.e. hunters, beaters and so forth. From this circumstance the custom described above becomes comprehensible as a survival from the common hunt when the game was shared among the participants.

The increase of cattle belonged to the owner of the parent cattle. The increase from stray cattle joining a Buriat's herds belonged to the owner of the herd if he had previously given notice of the fact that a stray had joined it (St. C., 131). The carcasses of cattle killed by wild beasts or drowned belonged to the owner of the cattle (St. C., 65,66).

Some embryos of the right of private property in immovables may generally be noted in Buriat law. The clan community had common pastures. Besides this, the clansmen had individual plots which were cultivated for hay (Ootougs) and also ploughlands. Good lands for haymows and ploughland were divided equally among the members of the clan. If, however, anyone fenced in a plot near his camp, cultivated it and irrigated it, such a plot did not come up for redivision but remained in his possession (C. of Sel. 8., 163).

The above provision demonstrates the labour character of the acquisition of individual plots. This is shown still more clearly by the following provision: "If anyone cultivates a plot of land for ploughing, or a haymow, and then does not use it and the fence falls into ruin and some one else wishes to use the fenced-in plot, then, if the first owner brings suit against him, he is to be given three years to cultivate the plot; if he fails to cultivate the land during this time, it becomes the property of the other who manifested his desire to make use of it; he has the right to fence it in but must, if possible, compensate the first owner for clearing the land (C. of Sel. B., 160, *cf*. C. of Verkh. B., 34,40).

We thus see that personal labour in the cultivation of land (and more particularly in irrigation which in the waterless steppe was a matter of especial difficulty) served as the basis for individual possession under Buriat law, but this possession was not yet fixed; and stoppage of cultivation could lead to the transfer of the plot to the possession of another for the same purpose. At the same time, it is evident that the origin of private property in immovables was connected with the transition to a more intensive economy, to the cultivation of land for haymows and ploughlands and to agriculture generally.

Responsibility for damages. Buriat law passed over to the fixing of responsibility (not only in criminal, but also in civil cases) on the principle of fault. Thus, according to the customs of the Southern Buriate, if cattle fell into a cutting in the ice made for them, no responsibility attached if the cutting was of proper width (2 chetvert = ½ yard), but if the cutting was greater than the established width, the person making it was answerable for the damage done (St. C., 99). If anyone, while catching a horse, collided with the horse of another and killed or crippled it, he was bound to make good the damage (St. C., 72). If anyone opened the gate of a fence and neglected to close it, he was held responsible for the damage (St. C., 129; C. of Sel. B., 166, etc.). Children (under eight years old) were not answerable for damage caused by them (St. C., 70). If anyone accidentally ran against a fence, the owner of the latter was not responsible for the damage (St. C. 94). If a labourer hired out for money died of disease or was crippled through his own carelessness, the master was not responsible (C. of Sel. B., 119) etc.

According to the customs of the Northern Verkholensk Buriats in cases of the trampling of fields by cattle, the owner of the cattle was liable for damages if the offence occurred through his negligence; but if the fence around the field was in bad condition, the owner of the fence was held responsible and the owner of the cattle was not considered responsible (C. of Verkh. B., 41,44).

However, besides these provisions fixing responsibility on the principle of fault (*culpa*), we meet with a series of provisions of private law in which the other (old) point of view (the causing) was applied but with diminution of responsibility.

Thus if anyone accidentally caused damage and loss to another, the damages were borne equally by both parties (C. of Hor. B., 11, 10). If anyone commissioned another to make a hilt for a knife, or a handle for an axe, and the other during his work accidentally cut himself or even died, the man who commissioned him was liable for two thirds of the expenses (St. C. 24, 25; C. of Hor. B., 11, 11) etc. If, during a hunt, an arrow struck another hunter, the man who shot it was obliged to make good the damage (St. C., 126).

Of contracts the most widespread among the Buriats were contracts without remuneration: gifts, loans, loadings, loans without interest (loans with interest being condemned), rent etc; and transactions with remuneration developed only gradually (47, 83 St. C.).

Inheritance in accordance with law (custom) prevailed in Buriat law.

In Buriat law the Will is met with as a supplement to inheritance by custom. Thus, according to the Customs of the Selenga Buriats: "If anyone have no wife or children nor brothers or relatives, but shall yet have a good superfluity, he must during his lifetime nominate a man who may use his property after his death.... and he must confirm this by a Will certified by the clan elders and leaders of the community." (C. of Sel. B., 133). According to the customs of the Horins and Selenguins Wills were permitted which named adopted children and wards as heirs (Steppe Code, 311; C. of Sel. B., 132) but according to the customs of the Selenguins these could in any case, and without a Will, inherit property on equal terms with the deceased's own children (C. of Sel. B., 131,136).

In general the civil life was not well developed but it was developed among Buriats more than among other native tribes.

Criminal Law: The criminal law of the Buriats was not complex. Formerly the criminal law of the Buriats was more severe[61] but it became gradually milder. After the Russian conquest serious criminal offences, such as murder, robbery and some others, were removed from the competence of the Buriat courts, being judged by Russian judicial organs. As a result of the simplicity of Buriat

61 In ancient time they used also the death-penalty.

life and the peace-loving nature of the people, such crimes were extremely rare. Of other crimes and offences the most important were personal insults and petty thefts. The penalties for insults varied with the social position of the insulter and insulted: the higher the position of the insulted person the more severe was the penalty and the higher the position of the insulter the greater the fine he had to pay. The penal system of the Southern Buriats was more complex, and the punishments it involved more severe than those applied by the Northern Buriats. Among them flogging with rods and the knout was practised, but generally speaking, both in the North and South, the main penalties were whipping and fines in kind.

Organization of the Court. According to the instruction of Count Ragusinsky of 1728, the judicial functions were discharged by the Ooloos Elder or clan Shulenga, assisted by six honourable clansmen. The final instance of appeal was the Chief Taisha who rendered decisions personally or in the Office. At this time there was no definite system of instances and generally no fixed principle of court organization. Investigation was conducted by tracking, universal search, and the questioning of witnesses. The oath was allowed.

By the terms of the Regulations of 1822 the clan administration (Executive Bureau) became the court of first instance, the second instance was the Steppe Council, and the third the local police. The final instance was the Russian district court. The competence of courts was precisely defined and definite rules of procedure were established.

6. JURISTIC CUSTOMS OF THE TUNGUSES

The Tungus tribes once occupied tremendous expanses of territory in Eastern Asia. They included, besides the Siberian Tunguses, the Manchus, the Solons, the Dauhurs, the Goldis, the Orochens, and a series of other tribes. The Su-shens (肅愼) and I-leus (挹婁) of the ancient Chinese chronicles were also supposed to be Tungus peoples. These tribes were noted for their warlike nature. On two occasions Tungus peoples ruled over north China (the Liao dynasty 遼 907-1125 A.D., and the Chin 金 1125-1234 A.D.), and in one case over the entire Chinese Empire (the Manchu dynasty, 1644-1911). In this article, however, we shall deal with the Tungus tribes proper or Siberian Tunguses.

At the beginning of the twentieth century Tunguses in Siberia numbered approximately 70,000. The majority of them were nomadic herdsmen inhabiting the region between Lake Baikal and the Lena as well as the Transbaikal. A part of them were wandering hunters who roamed through the forests of Northern Asia as far as the Sea of Okhotsk. About two thousand of them were settled ploughmen. Tunguses had a clan organization and were ruled by their clan elders under the supervision of Russian authorities (the Regulations of 1822). Courts were connected with the clan organization (in two first instances) and used the local customary law.

Records of Tungus Law.

1. The most ancient records of the customary law of the Tunguses are *The Ancient Juridical Customs of the Tunguses* which were first described by A. R. in an article, "Concerning the Laws of Some Siberian Natives" (printed in the *Siberian Messenger,* 1823, vol. I). These were presented in the form of 15 articles covering the spheres of civil and criminal law, together with some additional information concerning court organization. The origin of these customs is undoubtedly ancient but their codification could not have been very far back because of their reference to reckoning in Russian money — roubles (see art. 9). In Eastern Siberia Russian money is first mentioned in native legal documents of the second half of the eighteenth century, and for this reason the codification (i.e. the putting into writing), of the ancient juridical customs of the Tunguses must also be dated not earlier than the latter part of the eighteenth century. Information concerning these customs, given in the above-mentioned article by A. R., was repeated by Professor Leontovich in his work, *The Mongol-Oriat Regulations on Punishments* (1879, pp. 242-243).

2. *The Customs of the Tunguses of the Department of Nerchinsk* represents an account of the customs of the Tunguses of this region compiled on October 12, 1823 at the order of the Russian authorities who were then preparing the codification of the customary law of the native tribes of Siberia. These Customs comprise 68 articles, largely provisions of civil and criminal law with a small number of provisions regulating procedure. They were not divided into chapters and are printed in Professor Samokvasov's *Collection of the Customary Laws of the Siberian Natives* (1876, pp. 25-41).

3. *The Customs of the Tunguses of the Department of Prince Gantimurov*, comprise 88 articles and notes by Prince Gantimurov, including provisions of criminal and civil law. They were compiled at the same time as the Customs of the Nerchinsk Tunguses and for the purposes of the same codification. They were also printed in the above-mentioned work of Professor Samokvasov (pp. 43-66).

The Ancient Juridical Customs of the Tunguses (XVIIIc.)

1. "For the theft of cattle, the fine shall be four head of the same kind of cattle; and besides this, the culprit shall be subjected to corporal punishment (with rods)."

2. "The same measures shall be taken with anyone caught in any other kind of theft, from whom the stolen thing shall be taken or a sum of money equivalent in value to the stolen thing."

3. "An accomplice in a theft or one who knows of it and does not inform the headman is considered equal to the thief and shall be subjected to the same penalty."

4. "One caught cheating for the first time or a swindler shall be fined; if the offence is committed a second time the culprit shall be confined under guard for several days; and for the third time the culprit shall receive corporal punishment."

5. "Slanderers or persons bearing false witness shall be treated in the same manner."

6. "Anyone intentionally or maliciously killing or maiming cattle shall pay compensation for the damage and be subjected to corporal punishment."

7. "Disorderly behaviour, sloth, and insubordination to persons of higher rank will also be punished corporally."

8. "For drunkenness, after domestic means of correction have been applied, the culprit shall be sent away for labour."

9. "An elder clansman insulting a commoner by word or act will pay for the dishonour 5 roubles for the first time, 10 roubles for the second, and 15 roubles for the third."

10. "For maiming, this fine (for ordinary insult) shall be doubled, and the victim shall be cured at the expense of the culprit."

11. "Impoverished debtors shall be given to their creditors and remain in their hands until by their labours they shall have

paid the debt; or money shall be taken from them over a set period, depending upon their condition."

12. "When a marriage is dissolved by the mutual consent of both parties, the *kalim* (ransom paid by the groom for the bride) is not returned; on the contrary, the husband must give the wife a riding horse with harness and summer and winter clothing."

13. "When, however, the wife leaves her husband of her own will, the *kalim* given for her shall be taken back from her father or his heirs; or, if the husband consents, instead of this another maiden shall be given him."

14. "Whoever, after having been betrothed, refuses to take the bride to whom he is engaged shall forfeit his *kalim;* if, however, the parents or relatives of the bride refuse to give her to him in marriage, then the *kalim* shall be returned."

15. "All insults given behind a person's back shall be disregarded, as shall all crimes of minor importance concerning which no notice shall have been given within 6 days to the clan chief."

Concerning courts, Professor Leontovich gives the following information:

"The Shulengas (headmen of separate clans), when they receive complaints, summon together several elder clansmen and together they decide the case (this is evidently the court of old men)[62]. Important crimes are judged by the Chief Taisha (head of the tribe) in the Suglan clan conference, as among the Buriats. The accused (?) must appear in court with witnesses; if these do not exist and the accused contends his innocence, then his nearest clansmen are called who, in order to confirm the truth of the testimony, must in accordance with the ancient custom pronounce an oath before a gun or sword and in important cases upon the Shaman Stone (near the mouth of the Angara river). Enemies (of either party ?), minors and madmen are not admitted as witnesses" (*Op. cit.*, p. 243).

Contents of The Customs of The Tunguses (1823-1824)

Private Law: Property Law. — The Tunguses did not know the right of private property in immovables. Private property in

62 Probably a court of six elder clansmen in accordance with the permission granted by the Russian government that the natives might be judged by a native court of 6 elder clansmen (see *Instructions of Count Rayuzinsky.* 1728, etc.)

movables was, however, recognized. Hunting, fishing and cattle breeding were the chief occupations, though also agriculture to a small extent. The common pastures were divided into those used in summer and those used in winter. There also existed special haymows and sown fields. It was forbidden to wilfully occupy or take away a fenced-in winter field or summer camp site (*Customs of Nerchinsk Tunguses*, art. 52). It was prescribed that summer camps, haymows and fields were to be securely fenced (*Customs of Gantimurov Tunguses*, art. 58, 59). If one hunter wounded a beast and another killed it, the beast went to the first hunter; if anyone pursued a beast for a long distance and tired it out but another killed it, the carcass was divided equally among them (C O G T, 75). If anyone found money or anything in a field or vacant place he was obliged to declare this to the community. If the owner was found, the finder received one tenth of the value of the thing found. But if the finder hid the thing, then everything was given to the owner upon discovery while the concealer was subjected to corporal punishment and the informer received the one tenth (C O N T, 32; C O G T, 47). If dead cattle was found it was necessary to inform the people and it was possible to eat it after 3 days (C. O. G. T-49).

Law of Obligations. — Tungus law contained a number of provisions dealing with compensation for damage and loss. If damage was caused by a child under eight years of age, there could be no claim for compensation (C O N T, 25). If, while carrying a medicine man, anyone fell from his horse or sustained any other damage and loss, the driver was obliged by the Customs of the Nerchinsk Tunguses to pay half the expenses (art. 10) and according to the Customs of the Gantimurov Tunguses, one third (art. 18, 20). If a man riding on a horse or cart had a sharpedged weapon and someone asked the man to carry him and one of them sustained injury, then the second man paid 2/3 of the damage, but if the rider (driver) invited the second man to go with him, then he paid half the damage (C O N T, 13). If anyone sent another to break in an unridden horse and the man so sent fell and was crippled, the one who sent him was obliged to pay 2/3 of the expenses of healing and other losses, and if the man died he who sent him paid a horse for his soul (*Ibid.*, 11). If anyone gave another an axe or knife to sharpen and the latter crippled himself by his own mistake the responsibility was the same (*Ibid.*, 12). If a fire was caused (through negligence) in a house, haymow or field, the causer of the fire and the owner each bore half the loss; but if the fire was caused by other reasons, then the owner alone was obliged to pay all the loss (*Ibid.*, 40). Rabid dogs or cattle were to be killed; and if a mad animal suddenly escaped, notice was first to be given to the clan elder and published to all, otherwise the killer was answerable for the loss caused (*Ibid.*, 44). Whoever, during a great hunt, lost a horse or a camel, was to receive its cost from the company (C O G T, 30).

Old debts could be collected even after 30 or 40 years if certified in writing (*Ibid.*, 29); in the absence of such certification, collection could be made only within 15 years (*Ibid.*)[63] Persons taking goods on credit and not making payment on the date due were forced to pay, punishable with rods (*Ibid.*, 28). Creditors themselves were forbidden to seize their debtors' property for payment, and in case of the former doing so, the debt would be annulled and the creditors would be flogged (*Ibid.*, 30; C O G T, 40). It was forbidden to give a woman goods on credit without the knowledge of the master of the house; and any violation of this would subject the culprit to flogging; the debt however, had to be paid (C O N T, 48). To borrow and lend money was permitted only with the sanction of the clan chiefs; otherwise the interest was cancelled (*Ibid.*, 53). Among the Tunguses, as among the Buriats, gifts demanded similar gifts in return, and the return was to be equivalent in value to the original present (C O N T, 19), but if the receiver of the gift had notified the giver that he could return only a trifling present, this was permitted (C O G T, 27). The following contracts were practised: purchase and sale, loans and personal service; and the customs of the Tunguses provided for the fulfilment of these contracts according to conditions (C O N T, 64, 53, 55; C O G T, 37, 80).

The Family. — Marriages took place in accordance with a preliminary agreement concluded between the parents of the groom and bride with the payment of *kalim* (cattle) on the one hand and dowry on the other (C O N T, 15). If two fathers betrothed their respective children and one of them refused to give or take the bride, or one of the children died or was baptised but there were still other children left, then the cattle for the bride could once more be given (C O N T, 3). If a bride-groom who had paid full *kalim* died before the marriage, then one of his brothers or close relatives could marry the bride (C O G T, 9). Betrothal (marriage) "in exchange" also existed among the Tunguses, just as it did among the Buriats

63 In the Customs of the Tunguses of the Gantimurov Department, evidently under the influence of Russian law, the period of prescription was fixed at 10 years (art. 39).

(C O G T, 11 and supplement 3). A widow could live with her children on the property of her deceased husband, and if she wished to marry again, she had to take one of his relatives for a husband. If she wished to marry an outsider the consent of the clan elders was required (C O G T, 13). However, a widow could also return to her parents, in which case she could marry again at her own will (C O N T, 8). Polygamy existed and divorce was simple. A husband could leave his wife (*Ibid.*, 8, 9). A runaway wife would be returned to her husband (C O N T, 5, 7; C O G T, 66). But if the husband was impotent, insane or dead, she was permitted to leave him (C O N T, 7, 8). If a wife ran away more than once, the matter was referred to the clan elders for decision (*Ibid.*, 7).

Rich children were obliged to support impoverished parents (C O N T, 23) and younger brothers (C O G T, 23) and to marry off the latter (*Ibid.*, 22).

It was permitted to take a maid and to bring her up and she was regarded as a daughter(C O G T, 67). A grandfather could adopt his grandson (C O N T, 18) and bequeath property to him on the same terms as to his own children, including the father of the adopted child (*Ibid.;* C O G T, 24) ; and uncles could do the same with regard to their nephews (C O G T, 24).

Inheritance. — The "closest relatives" of man were his legal heirs (C O G T, 25). These included, it was indicated, brothers, children, grandchildren, great grandchildren, and descendants (C O N T, 17). Wills were permitted but only as a supplement to custom (see provisions on adoption above). If a man who had no close relatives willed his property to persons in another clan, estate was not handed over in accordance with the will and the matter was referred to the elders of his clan for decision (C O G T, 25). When a man died without heirs, one third of his property was devoted to memorial services and the reading of books over his grave, a third to the temple, and a third to the person who lived with him (C O N T, 17). According to the Customs of the Tunguses of the Department of Gantimurov, half of the property was paid for the reading of books over the grave, a quarter to the temple, and a quarter to the person who lived with the deceased before his death (art. 26).

Criminal Law: System of Punishments. — The following punishments were met with in Tungus customary law.

Beating with sticks (C O G T, 28, 42, 46.)

Whipping (C O N T, 31, 66, 67.)

Flogging with rods (C O N T, 49, 61; C O G T, 1, 3-5, 31, 72.)

Property fines (C O G T, 2, 41, 46, 88.)

Compulsory labour to pay off debts (C O G T, 28.)
These simple penalties applied, in accordance with the preliminary decision of the native courts, to the following crimes:

Crimes against Society and Morals. — It was forbidden to play cards or spin the teetotum for money, the punishment for so doing being flogging with rods (C O N T, 49; C O G T, 73). It was forbidden to lay wagers on pain of being flogged with rods, except on horses and with the permission of the officials (C O G T, 87). Persons under 30 years of age were forbidden to drink wine, except when offered by their wives' relatives; and clan elders were likewise forbidden to drink on pain of punishment (C O N T, 50). Drunken persons were forbidden to enter temples, and if they did so they were to be judged by the clan elders (C O G T, 6). Persons guilty of adultery were beaten with sticks and the man was obliged to give a horse to the offended husband (C O G T, 46).

Crimes against the Person: Severe Beating and Maiming. — If an elder serving as an official beat and maimed a clansman without cause, the culprit had to compensate the victim for damages and pay him a horse (C O G T, 2). The instigator of a fight in which anyone received maiming injury was obliged to pay for the cure of the victim for two months and pay him a horse, besides which he was flogged with rods (*Ibid.*, 3). If the instigator of the fight knocked out his opponent's eye, he was subjected to corporal punishment and had to pay his victim a horse and a cow with a calf. If the victim lost his sight completely, then the culprit was obliged to support him until death and also pay all taxes and levies on his behalf (*Ibid.*, 4). Anyone injuring another in the head was flogged with rods and obliged to pay the victim's medical expenses. Anyone tearing out the queue of another was obliged to pay the sufferer a two-year -old colt, besides which he was flogged with rods. For knocking out a tooth the culprit was flogged and paid the victim a three-year-old colt (*Ibid.*, 5).

Insults by word and Act. — Insults by word or act to Zaisans, Shulengas, Zazaouls and Lamas were judge by the superior clan chiefs and punished by flogging and property fines in accordance with the nature and magnitude of the insult. Insults to common

Huvaraks and clansmen were judged by the clan elders, and the defendant could appeal against the sentence of the elders to the superior chiefs (C O G T, 1). If sons (or daughters) cursed, swore at, or beat their parents, they were flogged with doubled severity. (C O G T, 31), at the presence of whole community and young generation in particular (C O N T, 22).

Slander. — If anyone slandered another and a quarrel, damage or loss resulted, the offender was whipped and obliged to pay the loss (C O N T, 31).

Crimes against Property: Theft. — Anyone stealing cattle, money, or things, was obliged to replace the things stolen and pay the costs of the tracing of the crime, besides which he was subjected to severe corporal punishment (C O N T, 66, 67). A thief having no possessions from which to replace what was stolen was given over (to the victim of the theft) for compulsory labour to cover the loss, besides which he was beaten with sticks or flogged with rods in accordance with the proportions of the crime (C O G T, 28). An uninvolved person discovering the thief was rewarded with 5 roubles which were taken from the culprit (C O G T, 44). Thieves were flogged with rods for the first offence and beaten with sticks for the second and third (*Ibid.*, 42). Anyone stealing a part of the kill during a hunt was flogged and fined a horse in favour of the loser (*Ibid.*, 83). If anyone took a fish from the line of another it was taken away from him and returned to its owner while the thief was punished with rods (C O G T, 72). Anyone stealing a beast from a trap, pit or loop had to pay a three-year-old head of cattle for each deer and roebuck, while for other beasts he had to pay their equivalent value. Besides this he was punished with rods (*Ibid.*, 84). If anyone witnessed a theft but did not catch the thief or report the matter and later charged the culprit with theft, giving details of where it was committed, he was forced to pay the loss involved in the theft and punished with rods (*Ibid.*, 78).

Court Organization and Procedure. Little information is available on the organization of courts among the Tunguses prior to the Regulations of 1822. Plaintiffs had first of all to apply to the clan elders. The clan elder could not refuse to consider a case, but if he was not sure of his own knowledge of the laws and customs involved he could invite neighbouring elders and reputable old men to be his assistants that they might decide the case together. Persons dissatisfied with the judgment of the elder could appeal to the superior chief or higher administrative office (C O N T, 58, 59, 60; C O G T, 1).

Tracking and search were applied as means of investigation and proof (C O N T, 68; C O G T, 42-47), as were also the questioning of competent persons and witnesses (C O N T, 62; C O G T, 82).

Sources of Tungus Law

Custom: The basic source of Tungus law lay in the customs of the Tunguses. At the base of their social relations was the patriarchal clan order, and their administration and judiciary were built on clan principles. Relationship was recognized in the male line. Marriage was exogamous and based on the purchase (ransoming) of the bride, polygamy being permitted. All these were institutions of customary law. Since the family was patriarchal in character, the power of the husband and father within the family was great, though not tyrannical. This is also an institution of customary law. In the same way the absence of the right of immovable property, the use of the land for purposes of cattle-breeding and hunting by clan unions, and the procedure of inheritance were also customary in character. The basic punishment in the penal system was the property fine, which is an institution of customary law, supplemented by flogging with rods and whips and compulsory labour to pay off debts. The simple crimes reflected the way of life of the Tunguses.

Mongol Law: Next in importance among the sources of Tungus law was Mongol law, the law of the Mongol tribes. The Tunguses once formed part of the Great Mongol Empire of Jenghiz Khan and later of one of the appanages of his sons into which the Empire split up. Still later, and until the most recent times, the Tunguses lived in close proximity to one of the Mongol tribes, the Buriats, and were under their cultural influence. The century-long subjection of the Tunguses first to the rule and then to the cultural influence of the stronger and more advanced Mongol tribes[64] could not but have an effect upon their law. It is necessary only to com-

64 Of the great influence of Buriat culture on the Tunguses we may judge from the following data. According to the census of 1897, no less than 4,878 Transbaikal Tunguses spoke Buriat as their native tongue and knew no other language. Of the Buriats in the region, only two gave Tungus as their native tongue (see Serebrennikov, "The Buriats", 1925, p. 13, note 2).

pare the legal customs of the Mongol tribes with those of the Tunguses to be convinced of the validity of this supposition.

For instance, Art. 4 of the Ancient Code of the Hori Buriats (1781) and Art. 61 of the Steppe Code (of the Hori Buriats) of 1808 punished adultery with the wife of another by the flogging of both the offenders and by taking a horse from the man in favour of the aggrieved husband. We meet analogous provisions in Art. 6 of the Customs of the Nerchinsk Tunguses and Art. 46 of the Customs of the Tunguses of the Department of Gantimurov, both the parties guilty of adultery being punished with rods and the offender fined a horse in favour of the offended husband. This method of fining the offender by a horse in favour of the husband did not arise from some common basis and was not met with among other nomadic tribes. It is our opinion that it was borrowed by the Tunguses from the Buriats. It is possible to prove that the fine of a horse taken from the offender in favour of the aggrieved husband in cases of adultery was an old Mongol custom. Thus we meet this custom in the Ancient Tsaadjin Bichik (fifteenth century), Art. 3, and in the customary law of Autonomous Mongolia. It is difficult to assume that the Tunguses of the fifteenth century, who were far away from Mongolia and especially from Western Mongolia, and were weaker and less cultured than the Mongols, could influence the Ancient Tsaadjin Bichik and Mongol law in general in this respect. It is more natural to consider that it was ancient Mongol customs that influenced Tungus law through the law of the Buriats.

Let us quote another example. To acquire wives by means of purchase was an ancient custom, connected with nomadic patriarchal culture. In a milder form this custom was practised among the nomadic tribes of Central Asia, e.g. in the payment of *kalim* for the wife. Among the Mongols[65] and Buriats, however, a special form of marriage was developed as a deviation from the *kalim*—the "anda" marriage, or "mutual" marriage of the Southern Buriats (*cf.* Steppe Code, 14; Customs of the Hori Buriats, VI, etc.) or the marriage "in exchange" of the Northern Buriats (Customs of the Verkholensk Buriats-18, Customs of the Idinsk, Tunkinsk and Kudinsk Buriats, VI). Under this definition was understood the mutual marriage of two couples from two families: a son of the first father with a daughter of the second, and a daughter of the

65 *v.* Khalkha Djirum (Riasanovsky-Fundamental Principles of Mongol Law, 1937, p. 239).

first with a son of the second, i.e., a son and daughter of one family to the daughter and son of a second (son, grandson, nephew—daughter, granddaughter, niece, etc.). We meet this phenomenon also among the Gantimurov Tunguses. Art. 11 of the Customs of the Gantimurov Tunguses reads: "It also happens that according to our faith the agreement can be concluded without payment of cattle *in exchange*, when one takes from another a daughter for a son..." (*cf.* also supplement to C O G T, 3). Thus the question arises as to what we have here: a borrowing or rather the independent occurrence of analogous customs? Among the Buriats this custom was more developed and was worked out fully in their juridical records. It was met with among the Northern and Southern Buriats under different names. Among the Tunguses it was less developed and was found only in the customs of the Department of Gantimurov, the inhabitants of which were the neighbours of the Northern Buriats and called the marriage by the same name as the latter. In view of the foregoing, we may conclude that the Gantimurov Tunguses borrowed this form of marriage from their neighbours, the Northern Buriats.

We may notice such an influence of the customs of the stronger and more cultured Mongol tribes on the customs of the less cultured Tungus tribes (of Nerchinsk and Gantimurov) in a whole succession of instances.

For example, Art. 40 of the Steppe Code embodies the regulation that a child under 8 years of age bears no responsibility for harm and damage inflicted by him in the course of his games. "If a minor child should cause some grievance or damage in the course of his games, and if the child is less than 8 years of age, such grievance or damage shall be left without consequences" (Art. 40, Steppe Code). We come across the same regulation in Art. 25 of the Customs of the Nerchinsk Tunguses: "If anyone's child in the course of voluntary games, should cause damage or trouble, and if the said child should be less than 8 years of age, such damage or trouble shall be left unremedied." Both these regulations are closely analogous and appear to repeat each other. Here we see not only the age at which there is no disposing capacity coincides, but also the same detail (reservation) that the damage must be caused in the course of the child's play. It is difficult to consider such coincidences as purely fortuitous. Evidently we are dealing with borrowed customs.

The Steppe Code (Art. 48) and the Customs of the Nerchinsk Tunguses (Art. 29) contain respectively analogous regulations of prescription:

> "If there was an ancient debt due from someone and if there was a document respecting it, or witnesses, then it was necessary to recover it even if 30 or 40 years had passed. But if there were no documents or witnesses, then such cases were to be decided within a period of 15 years" (Steppe Code, 48).

> "If someone has a debt due to him, even if 30 or 40 years have passed, as long as there is a written receipt and witnesses, it can be recovered. But in case there are no letter or witnesses, there must be an investigation respecting it if more than 15 years have elapsed" (C O N T, 29).

Even though the meaning of the closing words of the latter regulation is not quite clear, still there can be no doubt respecting the borrowing.

The Customs of the Hori Buriats (Chap. IX, Art. 13) embody provisions respecting found articles. If anyone found goods or money lost on the road, he had to notify the clan chief or the clansmen; if the owner was found, the finder received 1/10 of the value of the thing found; but if the owner was not found within a period of three years, the thing found became the property of the finder; if the finder concealed the fact of its finding, the article had to be returned and the finder was flogged, while the reward of 1/10 was given to the person proving the concealment. The Customs of the Nerchinsk Tunguses (Art. 32) contain an analogous regulation though there is no indication of the three year period. But here also the finder was entitled to 1/10 of the value of the thing found; and the concealment of the found article was also punished by flogging, while any person proving concealment also received a reward of 1/10 the value of the thing. Here it is of course impossible to establish a common basis in the 1/10 reward for the finder and the same reward to persons reporting the concealment. The borrowing of the custom in general (with some omissions) is evident.

Thus we have presented several Buriat customs which were repeated among the Tunguses not only in basic principles but also in the secondary details. This, taken as a whole, gives us the right to speak not only of the coincidence of such customs but of borrowing by the Tunguses from the more powerful and cultured

Buriat tribes which influenced them greatly both through conquest and close neighbourhood.

But we must stress that we have not by far made use of all the material at our disposal. For example, the regulations contained in Art. 69 of the Steppe Code and Art. 52 of the Customs of the Gantimurov Tunguses (regarding giving cattle into the herds of another) are analogous, as are Arts. 29 and 30 of the Customs of the Selenga Buriats and Art. 49 of the Customs of the Gantimurov Tunguses (on the finding of cattle which has been torn to pieces by wolves); Art. 39 of the Steppe Code and Art. 24 of the Customs of the Nerchinsk Tunguses (on the giving up of a son to be brought up by another); Art. 91 of the Steppe Code and Art. 67 of the Customs of the Gantimurov Tunguses (on giving up a daughter to be brought up by another); Art. 31 of the Steppe Code and Art. 18 of the Customs of the Nerchinsk Tunguses (on the adoption of a grandson); Art. 4 of the Hipp Toktogol of 1788 and Art. 9 of the Customs of the Gantimurov Tunguses (on the death of a bridegroom before marriage); Art. 30 of the Steppe Code and Art. 17 of the Customs of the Nerchinsk Tunguses (on escheats); Arts. 8, 9, and 10 of the Ancient Code of 1781 and 50 and 51 of the Steppe Code and Arts. 1, 2 and 3, of the Ancient Customs of the Tunguses (eighteenth century) on theft. So also Arts. 25, 46, 33 of the Steppe Code, Art. 34, of the Customs of Selenginsti Buriats and Arts. 13, 28, 20 of Customs of Nerchinsk Tunguses and Art. 57 Customs of Gantimurov Tunguses.

In the same way, it is necessary to mention that, apart from the above, similar customs existed among the Buriats and Tunguses of which the origin among the latter may be explained not only by borrowings from the Buriats but also by other causes, particularly from the point of view of independent origin due to the similarity of the two cultures. Compare, for example, the provisions of Arts. 31 and 44 of the Customs of the Nerchinsk Tunguses and Arts. 42, 50 and 81 of the Customs of the Gantimurov Tunguses with the similar Arts. 63, 17, 52, 66 and 109 of the Horin Steppe Code of 1808.

Thus, on the basis of the material examined above, we come to the conclusion that the customs and law of the Mongol, and in particular, of the Buriat tribes, influenced to a considerable extent the customs and law of the Tunguses who were long subject to the Mongols and later lived in close neighbourhood with them.

Russian Law: Russian law also exercised a certain influence on the laws of the nomadic tribes of Siberia, among them Tungus law. The Tunguses were conquered by the Russians in the second half of the 17th century, and Russian influence was first of all felt in the sphere of the administrative organization of the native tribes. The Russian authorities confirmed the positions of the superior clan chiefs: Taishas, Princes, distributed rewards, paid salaries, and gave the tribes a certain measure of administrative organization in the interests of efficient government and the collection of duties and levies. At the beginning of the nineteenth century the Russian authorities organized the administration and judiciary of the native tribes of Eastern Siberia on the basis of certain definite principles based on the clan organization of these tribes (*See The Regulations (Statute) Concerning the Administration of the Native Tribes of Eastern Siberia, 1822,* — clan offices, native administrative bureaus, Steppe Dumas, etc.). The court organization was connected with the native clan administration (the first two instances, the clan office and native administrative bureau, being purely native, while the third was the district police station and the fourth the Russian District Court). In the sphere of material law, the Russian power at the beginning of the eighteenth century (See *Instruction of Count Raguzinsky, 1728*) removed the major criminal offences from the competence of the native courts of Eastern Siberia and also prohibited the application of the death penalty, maiming punishments and torture. Apart from this, however, the Russian authorities did not directly interfere with the contents of the native customary law, permitting the nomads to consider cases in accordance with their "steppe laws and customs." The Russian Government made an attempt to codify these steppe laws and customs[66]. Moreover, the influence of Russian law which was framed for a people of higher culture, could not fail to affect directly the material law of the native tribes of Siberia, and of the Tunguses in particular. Thus, in connection with the development of a money economy there appeared among the Tunguses the usage of reckoning in Russian roubles and copecks, as for example the payment of money instead of cattle fines for personal insults (Art. 9 of the Ancient Customs of the Tunguses) and some other cases (*cf.* CONT, 24). The Russian ten-year prescription was also applied (COGT, 39). So also under Russian influence there developed

66 *v.* further, 8. The author has in his possession a copy of the will of the Tungus Virpai Orosin of the Ezhansk clan dated December 9, 1755. Russian influence is evident from the form of this "oral letter".

rent of immovable property and credit transactions (see for instance, C O N T, 29, 53; C O G T, 80, etc.). The will also came into existence[67] (C O N T, 18; C O G T, 25).

Basic Features of Tungus Customary Law

The social structure of the Tunguses was based on the clan-patriarchal order. They were divided into clans (over 70 in all) which usually bore the name of the senior clansman. At the head of each clan stood an elder or Daruga, at the head of 2 or 3 clans a Zaisan. Several related clans formed a tribe headed by a Noyon or tribal prince. Families descended directly from the founder of the clan comprised a privileged class, the nobility; and from their midst were elected the Darugas and Zaisans, of whom one was promoted to the status of Noyon. Litigations and disputes were settled by the clan elders, alone or with the participation of honourable clansmen.

Family organization, in its fundamental features, was also based on clan-patriarchal culture. Relationship was recognized in the male line. Marriage was exogamous, i.e. alliances between members of the same paternal clan were not permitted, though this principle began to be weakened in recent times. Polygamy was permitted. Marriages were effected by the purchase or ransoming of the bride (*kalim*) and the giving of dowry (C O N T, 15). Marriage "in exchange" was also practised among the Tunguses. In such cases no *kalim* was paid but the son of one family married the daughter of another while the son of the latter married the daughter of the first (C O G T, 11). Actually polygamy was not widespread. Divorce was extremely simple and could take place not only by mutual consent but also by unilateral desire. In the latter case it was followed by a property settlement (return of the *kalim* and the dowry) which varied in accordance with the measure of guilt of one or the other of the parties (C O N T, 7-9).

The power of the father, lord of the family, was very great, as was that of parents generally. The power of the father dominated in the family during his lifetime. The marriages of children were arranged by the parents without seeking the youngsters' consent. Inheritance was determined in accordance with custom, the chief heirs being the sons, and children still with the family having

67 *cf.* also Art. 58 C. O. G. T. (the feast of Holy Virgin).

greater rights than those who had separated themselves from it. Wills were permitted only as a supplement to custom.

Civil transactions were but weakly developed. Credit transactions appeared late, chiefly in connection with the spreading of money economy and under Russian influence.

In the sphere of criminal law, within the limits fixed for the competence of the local native courts, one may note the mildness of the penalties and the simplicity of the crimes provided for as being characteristic of the simple Tungus life. Among the punishments, the property fine, predominantly in cattle, was fundamental, while the chief crimes provided for were personal insults and simple theft.

7. JURISTIC CUSTOMS OF THE YAKUTS.

Records of Yakut Law.

The Yakuts are a Turki tribe inhabiting Northern Central Asia — the middle and lower reaches of the Lena river and the shores of the Arctic Ocean. At the beginning of the twentieth century the Yakuts numbered about 250,000. This tribe originally came from the South and has preserved in its language many Mongol and Turki words. Yakut tradition concerns references to their "czar Jenghiz."

The Yakuts were divided into clans, Naslegs and Oolooses with the elder clansmen in the head [clan-elders, native princes, etc.] "The Regolations regarding the Administration of Siberian Natives" of 1822 were applied to the Yakuts.

"The Customs of the Yakuts" are printed in Prof. Samokvasov's "Collection of the Customary Laws of the Siberian Natives", 1876, pp. 199-243. They consist, in this work, of 144 articles divided into 31 chapters. The titles of the chapters are as follows: I. On Sacrifices; II. On the Composition of the Yakut Administration; III. On Entering Service; IV. On the Maintenance of the Steppe Administration; V. On Judicial Procedure; VI. On Placing under Guard; VII. On Disobedient Persons; VIII. On Unquiet Yakuts and Those Intolerable in the Clans; IX. Offenders; X. On Affairs Connected with the General Structure of an Entire Nasleg; XI. On Places Possessed by the Yakuts and the Profits Thereof; XII. On Shamanism; XIII. On Polygamy; XIV. On Kalim; XV. On Insults; XVI. On Thefts of All Kinds; XVII. On Things Found; XVIII. On Lechery; XIX. On False

Actions; XX. On Gambling with Dice; XXI. On Drunkenness; XXII. On Fugitives and Vagrants; XXIII. On the Feeding of the Poor; XXIV. On Inheritance; XXV. On Debts; XXVI. On the Care and Pasturing of Cattle: XXVII. On Veterinary Practice: XXVIII. On Hiring Workers; XXIX. On Gifts; XXX. On Conditions and Agreements; XXXI. On the Causing of Steppe Fires (Pals).

The year of the compilation of the "Customs of the Yakuts" is not given, but they were grouped with the materials for the codification referred to above and we may therefore refer them to the year 1823 (or 1824).

Juridical Customs of the Yakuts Codified in the Beginning of the XIXth Century.

Private Law.

Property Law. — The Yakuts did not know individual property in land. The land was in the possession and disposal of the Oolooses (e.g. the forests) or the Naslegs (e.g. pastures and haymow.) The Yakuts of one Nasleg had no right to camp on the pastures of another. Separate clansmen were not permitted to fence off part of the pastures for their own cattle. But, with the permission of the clan officials, they were permitted to make clearings, drain marshes, and fence off haymows in forest or pasture land and use such plots apart from the other clansmen for 10 years "as a reward for their labours and expenses." Haymows were divided into plots among the clansmen, and in the distribution of these plots due regard was given to "the ancient possessions of ancestors, so that these pass to the sons etc." But these haymows could also become smaller with the growth of population, for the purpose of providing for those not having plots, as a consequence of flooding, etc. Masters of haymows had the right to construct buildings upon them and plant orchards and were obliged to fence off their plots with strong and lasting fencing. With the knowledge of the clan officials it was permitted to rent out haymows ("Kortoma") or to mortgage them for a period not exceeding 4 years (XI).

Anyone catching a runaway animal or finding something was obliged to report it to the clan authorities, or at any rate to his neighbours, within three days. If the owner of the found thing or animal turned up, the finder received a reward "in the measure of his labours and expenses" but in no case exceeding one quarter of the value of what was found. If the finder failed without good cause to report the thing found within 3 days, be received no reward; and if he concealed his find entirely he was treated in the same way as a thief (XVII).

If a hunter when chasing a beast stops, then another hunter, after the lapse of 3 days, may chase the beast and kill it for his own use; if, however, he does so before the 3 days he receives half the beast or its value; equally so does the person who renders aid to the hunter (or who gives him a fresh horse) receives a part of the killed beast, depending on the extent of the help rendered (XI).

Law of Obligations. — Agreements and contracts, both written and oral, were accepted as the basis on which cases could be decided. In cases of dispute, oral contracts could be proved by witnesses, or in the absence of these by the oath (XXX). Loan obligations were allowed both with documentary certification and without. Interest was paid on monetary loans either in money or in the form of deliveries of firewood, hay, butter, cattle, fish, etc. For the non-payment of debts within the stipulated time a special fine for the infringement of contract was collected, together with interest and damages. Loan of cattle, food, hay, firewood, etc. was also practiced with repayment in kind after a set period. In case of non-payment in time the cattle were seized with increase and milk products. Horses and oxen were hired out for use for definite periods for agreed compensation in money (XXV). The custom was widespread among the Yakuts of "boarding out" cattle, usually for a year, for an agreed amount (from 20 to 40 head to each family). For the upkeep of 20 head of horned cattle for a year the payment was 20 roubles in money, 4 cows for meat and one ox for haulage. In return for this, the person undertaking the upkeep of the cattle was obliged to take it out to pasture in summer and feed it on hay during the winter; the products of milking (in butter and sour milk) were to be delivered to the owner in the autumn (besides the milk and products from the cattle boarded out).

Labourers were hired orally. A labourer did not have the right to serve two masters at the same time, and it was not permitted to entice a worker away from his master. If a worker was enticed during the hay-mowing season, the offender was obliged to pay the first employer as much hay as one worker usually mowed during a summer. A worker could be punished with rods on the complaint of his owner for idleness, negligence and disobedience. If an employer overworked a labourer, fed him worse than was usual among the Yakuts, cursed him constantly or, especially, beat him, he was also punished in the measure of his offence (XXVIII). If a man contracted to build or make anything and failed to complete the work and ran away, the article or building was completed at the expense of the fugitive who was forced to pay the loss and was punished by being confined under guard (XXVIII).

The practice of making gifts was highly developed among the Yakuts, as a sign of friendship and in the hope of receiving a gift in return, which was required. A Yakut receiving a present often returned one of greater value in the hope of making another visit and receiving a new present in return, and such mutual gifts continued until the gifts of both sides were equal. But misunderstandings and disputes often arose as to who had given more and who was obliged to add something. Such disputes were often decided by the courts on the following basis: the Yakut in debt was obliged to give back money without interest, cattle without increase or milk, and horses without Tels (Tel was a money payment for the hire of horses and oxen: 14 to 25 roubles per year for a horse, 3 to 5 roubles for an ox). (XXIX-2). There were, however, gifts which did not demand return and were given without the intention of receiving any compensation (XXIX-3). Only these last represented gifts in the juridical sense.

If the owner of a hay meadow fences it off badly, and the cattle of another enters and damages the grass, the owner of such cattle is not responsible for the damage. If a person who passes through the hay meadow opens and then does not close the gate, he is responsible for damage caused by cattle (XI-9...).

If cattle died as a consequence of neglect, the person in whose care it was had to pay compensation in money or in kind, but he did not answer for deaths caused by epidemics or for missing cattle in case the thief who stole them was discovered. If he employed the cattle for his own profit without the agreement of the owner he was forced to pay its cost and was moreover flogged for wilful abuse (XXVI-1,2).

Family Law. — Marriage. Among the Yakuts a Kalim, the amount of which was agreed between the parties, was paid for the bride, usually in cattle but sometimes in money. The parents or clansmen of the bride provided a dowry in cattle, clothing, and sometimes money, amounting to not less than half of the amount of the Kalim but sometimes equal to or even exceeding the entire amount. At the wedding the bridegroom made presents of cattle, money or skins to the bride's relatives. For this, the wife with her retinue returned to her family shortly after the marriage and collected return gifts of not less than ten head of cattle or thrice the amount of the first gift from them. Any excess in the cost of the return gifts was added to the Kalim. At divorce, the wife or her relatives returned the Kalim to the husband after deducting the dowry and excess of return gifts. Thus the Yakut wife (as was noted in the Customs of the Yakuts) had no property if her dowry did not exceed the amount of the Kalim or if she did not receive property in the form of a gift from her relatives after marriage (XIV). Polygamy was allowed among the Yakuts but not more than 5 wives were permitted one time. The causes of polygamy were as follows: The betrothal of children at an early age and consequent loveless marriages giving rise to the necessity for a second marriage for love; serious illness of the wife making it impossible for her to attend to her duties in the household (rich Yakuts having households at several points had several wives to look after different branches of their economy), etc, (XIII). Divorce was extremely simple and was permitted by mutual consent or unilateral wish. A husband could leave his wife for loose conduct, bad management of his household, or simply from dislike. A husband leaving his wife for no good reason did not receive back his Kalim but had to return the wife's dowry. A wife leaving her husband because of cruel treatment had the same rights as one left by her husband without good cause. A wife leaving her husband without good cause or because of dislike for him had to return the Kalim, i.e. her relatives had to return the Kalim paid for her. The husband's relatives had no right to force his widow to re-marry, but she herself, if she did not wish to remain in her husband's family, could re-marry without Kalim (XIV).

Well-to-do brothers already separated from the parental household were obliged to support and marry off poor brothers who had not yet set up their own households (XIV).

Inheritance. — All children of both sexes born of legally married or unmarried wives taken for Kalim were considered legitimate and had equal rights to the inheritance, which was divided equally among unmarried children of both sexes. Married sons and daughters already married off and endowed had no right to the inheritance. But if all the sons and daughters were married, only the sons inherited. If there were no sons, the married daughters received one head of cattle each while the rest of the property went to collateral relatives. If a man had no children (or only married daughters) his property went to his blood brothers and nephews. After the death of her husband a widow received the excess of her dowry over the Kalim, if such excess existed, and a quarter of the husband's property. A husband could will to his wife all property acquired by his own efforts, but property which he himself inherited went to his children and closest relatives (XXIV).

Criminal Law.

System of Punishments. — The system of punishments among the Yakuts was very simple. The following penalties were applied:

Exile for settlement in Okhotsk and Kamchatka (VIII);

Deprivation of the right to participation in civil life (IX).

Flogging (XV, XVI, XXI);

Arrest in stocks (VII, VI).

Arrest in fetters (VI).

Arrest (XIX, XX);

Property and money fines (XV);

Reprimand (XXI);

Giving away into service (XVI, XXII, XXV).

The crimes and offences subject to the jurisdiction of the native Yakut courts were also not complex.

Crimes against Society and Morals. — Disorderly Yakuts and those who could no longer be tolerated in the clans (persons caught in their fourth theft, loose drunkards, persons failing to pay their debts as a result of dishonest combinations, disrespectful persons and those guilty of insubordination to the clan elders, calumniators, etc.) were handed over to the administration for despatch to Okhotsk and Kamchatka for settlement there (VIII). Dishonoured persons (i.e. those punished for theft, deprived of positions, caught giving false witness, loose livers) were not asked to attend community meetings nor were they called upon to hold office or given a vote in public affairs (IX). Persons spreading false rumours and libels against the good name of others were punished by being reprimanded or put under arrest; perjurers and persons giving false information were punished by reprimand, arrest or flogging depending upon the seriousness of the offence, besides which they were liable for any damage caused (XIX). Constant drunkards were punished by reprimands and arrest and persons starting a brawl while in a drunken state were arrested or flogged (XXI). Gambling at cards or dice for money or things was forbidden and was punished by arrest, and if accompanied by brawling or disorderly conduct—by flogging (XX).

For the rape of a married woman or maid and upon her complaint the offender was subjected to corporal punishment with rods and made to pay dishonour (see below). Cases of adultery were considered by the clan officials who brought about a reconciliation of the married couple while the adulterer was flogged. If a husband caught his wife with another, the latter, besides being flogged, also paid dishonour. Whoever led astray a married woman or a betrothed maid so that the husband or bridegroom refused to take her back was forced to pay the husband or bridegroom the Kalim paid for the woman (XVIII).

Crimes Against the Person. — Mayhem and heavy beating. Persons guilty of mayhem or heavy beating paid dishonour and covered the victim's medical expenses as well as the cost of hiring a labourer to do the victim's work during the period of his incapacitation (XV, 4).

Insults by word and act. For insults by act the following fines for dishonour were paid: for insulting the headman of a clan—a horse worth 100 roubles and a feast of one carcass of cattle and one vessel containing Koumiss to a total value of 150 roubles; for insulting a princeling—cattle, money and things to the value of 50 roubles. If, however, the headman of the clan refused to be satisfied with the fine for dishonour paid him, the offender was flogged. For insults to the wives and daughters of clan officials the offenders paid double. Insults to common clansmen and the sons of clan officials were punished with a fine equivalent to the amount the insulted person contributed to the clan treasury and community during one year. If the insult was offered in public the offender paid not only dishonour but also an additional fine of 10 roubles for insulting a clan official and 5 roubles for a common Yakut. For personal insult by word of mouth the dishonour and fines paid were half of those listed above. Swearing at a man behind his back was not punished. Cases of insults to parents by their children were usually solved by reconciliation, but if forgiveness was not given the children were punished at the will of their parents (XV).

Crimes Against Property. — Robbery. Armed robbery with violence, beating and mayhem was tried by the general State court. Unarmed seizure of a thing without further violence was tried by the native administrative offices and the culprits were punished by flogging and forced to return the stolen things and pay all losses (XVI).

Theft. Anyone stealing cattle for the first time paid for it fourfold, and if the stolen cattle were found, three head for each one stolen and all expenses connected with the tracking down of the crime. If, however, the culprit had previously been involved in criminal affairs he was also subjected to corporal punishment. For second and third thefts the culprits were also flogged. After the third theft they were, by the sentence of the court, expelled from their Naslegs and exiled to the Okhotsk or Kamchatka region or handed over, under guarantee, to their families. Fourth offenders were exiled. Persons stealing money or things paid their cost and the loss involved and besides this were flogged. After the third theft they were treated as stated above. Accomplices and concealers of thefts were treated as thieves (XVI). In swindling thefts of cattle the stolen animals were replaced head for head but the culprit was flogged even for the first offence (XVI).

Arson and Steppe Fires. Before setting fire to his own plot every Yakut was obliged to give notice to his neighbours so that they might take precautionary measures, otherwise the causer of the Pal (steppe fire) was liable for any loss incurred. If anyone left an unextinguished fire in a field or forest or negligently handled fire in the neigbourhood of buildings, he was responsible for any damage arising from his action (XXXI). Premeditated arson of buildings was tried by the general State courts (XXXI, note).

Court Organization and Procedure.

Before the promulgation of the Regulations of 1822, important and complicated litigations, e.g. in connection with large thefts, disputed camp sites, etc., were considered in accordance with the instructions of Count Razumovsky (1728) by a court of 6 clan officials. Against the judgment of this court there was no appeal. In connection with less important litigations between clansmen, the claims were presented to the clan elders and Nasleg princes, and in case of dissatisfaction with their verdict to the heads of the Oolooses, and finally to the Russian administrative offices.

Upon a claim being received, the defendant was summoned and if he admitted the claim the affair ended with an award to the plaintiff. If, however, he did not recognize the justice of the claim, witnesses were questioned (under oath). In the absence of witnesses the case was decided in accordance with the statements under oath of one of the parties. If both sides agreed to a settlement by oath, the preference was given to the plaintiff (V).

If an Yakut after receiving three notifications from the clan officials does not appear without lawful cause, then, if he has been summoned in connection with a claim of a private individual, he is considered to be guilty of the offence imputed to him; if he has been summoned in connection with treasury or public affairs, then, if he is not an ordinary clansman, he is punished by being kept under guard in stocks, and an ordinary clansmen is punished by beating with rods and payment to the messengers bringing the summons (VII-I).

According to the Regulations of 1822 the first two instances of Courts were purely native, and the last two instances were Russian, but local customary law was applied in all instances.

Sources of Yakut Law.

The sources of Yakut law comprised, in the order of their importance, custom, Mongol law, and Russian law.

Custom. — The juridical customs of the Yakuts were the chief source of Yakut law. Here, too, we meet the patriarchal clan order serving as the basis of the administration and the courts. Relationship was recognized through the father. Marriage was exogamous and polygamy was permitted (but with not more than 5 wives). All these were institutions of customary law. The family was patriarchal in character. The power of the husband and father in the family was great but not despotic. Inheritance was governed by custom. The absence of the right of private property in immovables, the common use of the land by the clans for purposes of cattle-breeding and the apportioning of plots for haymows were all institutions of customary law. In the same way the main penalties, (property fines in cattle, flogging and delivery into forced labour), as well as the simple crimes were regulated by custom, as were in general the organization of the courts and judicial procedure.

Mongol Law. — Mongol law also exerted an influence on the law of the Yakuts, although this influence was less pronounced than in the case of Tungus law.

It is necessary to bear in mind the fact that the Yakuts, once comprised a part of the Mongol Empire and were compelled to retreat from the South to the North by the Mongol tribes approximately in the fourteenth or fifteenth centuries. Some of the Yakut regulations concerning theft, divorce and the payment of Kalim show common characteristics with the corresponding regulations of the Buriats.

Thus, art. 8 of the Ancient Code of the Hori Buriats (1781) provided that "for the theft of cattle, the so-called Yal is imposed, which rules that for each stolen head of cattle three more of the same kind, from 2 to 4 years old, must be given. Moreover, the culprit is liable to corporal punishment."

According to the Customs of the Idinsk and Balagansk Buriats, four head of cattle had to be given for each one stolen (supplemented by corporal punishment in the case of second theft—C. of Bal. & Id. B., V. I), while third theft was punished by exile (*Ibid.*).

The Customs of the Yakuts contain analogous provisions. Thus, anyone committing theft for the first time paid four similar animals for each head stolen, while if the stolen animal was recovered alive he returned it and paid three others, also compensating the owner for any losses suffered; and thieves who had previously committed any evil actions were subjected to corporal punishment (XVI, 3); for the second theft flogging was obligatory; and after the third theft the culprit was considered incorrigible and exiled (XVI, 4). Not only the basic rule that cattle thieves were to be punished by fines in cattle (Yal) and the amount of the multiple fine were identical in the case of both the Buriats and the Yakuts, but also supplementary details.

Furthermore, the Steppe Code of the Hori Buriats (art. 51) stated: "If anyone commit theft of goods or anything else and the stolen articles are not found, the thief must be forced to pay the actual value of the goods and be severely flogged with the knout." In the Customs of the Selenga Buriats (Chap. I, art. 5) we find the following provision in this connection: "If anyone steal anything from another and the theft be uncovered, the articles are to be returned in kind; but if the article has been used by the thief then let it be evaluated and let the cost be collected from the culprit who is moreover to be dealt with in accordance with the first paragraph.[68] And if the owner of the article has borne any losses as a consequence of the theft, these are, in accordance with the circumstances and the demands of justice, to be collected from the thief."

68 Punishment by rods (v. art. 1) and, in case of inability to pay, compulsory service (art. 4).

Analogous provisions are found in Yakut law: "For money and things the thief pays not fourfold but the value of what was stolen, with the losses which as a result of his theft have been suffered by the owner of the stolen money and goods; besides this he is punished corporally with rods, irrespective of whether the amount stolen is small or great" (XVI, 5).

From the data given one may see the close resemblance, almost identity, of the Buriat and Yakut provisions regarding theft, which forces us to assume that borrowing by the Yakuts from the Buriats took place. This is confirmed by the fact that the Buriats were the more cultured and the stronger tribe as well as by the data given below. In the ancient law of the Tunguses (eighteenth century) we find analogous provisions regarding theft, i.e. cattle-thieves were obliged to pay fourfold for stolen cattle and were punished with rods, while a thief stealing other articles was obliged to return them or replace their value, being also punished with rods.[69] Thus we find the same provisions regarding theft among the Buriats, Tunguses and Yakuts. It is evident that they all stemmed from one and the same source. The only such common source could be Mongol, and particularly Buriat, law, in which the Yal was the basic and most widespread punishment met with in the eighteenth and nineteenth centuries among both Northern and Southern Buriats. The Tunguses borrowed this custom (with other customs) from the Buriats and it came to the Yakuts through their Tungus neighbours as well as directly from the Buriats.

Other provisions analogous among the Yakuts and Buriats were those relating to divorce. Here we meet the possibility of divorce by the unilateral desire not only of the husband but also of the wife, as well as analogous provisions concerning the property settlement consequent upon divorce. For instance, according to the Customs of the Selenga Buriats, if the divorce transpired as a result of the husband's reluctance to continue living with his wife, he had not the right to demand the return of his Kalim and was obliged to send away his wife "with good clothing and outfitting" (C. of Sel. B., 49). The same applied to divorce resulting from cruelty on the part of the husband (*Ibid., 42*). We find analogous provisions among the Yakuts: "A husband leaving his wife without any cogent motive does not receive his Kalim but, on the contrary, gives her dowry, clothing and apparel, ornaments and things; and this right is also

69 Leontovich, "Ancient Mongol-Kalmuck or Oirat Regulations on Punishments", 1879, p. 142, arts. 1,2., v. above, pg. 73.

possessed by a wife leaving her husband as a result of cruel or bad treatment" (XIV, 5).

On the basis of the above we may conclude that the law of the Mongol tribes to a certain extent influenced not only the military-administrative organization of the Yakuts, but also their private and criminal law.

Russian Law.—Russian law also exerted great influence in the spheres of administration and the organization of the courts (Regulations of 1822). Certain important crimes were removed from the competence of the local (Yakut) courts, but apart from these exceptions the Russians did not interfere in the spheres of the material, criminal and civil, law of the Yakuts. However, the influence of both Russian culture and Russian law affected in certain respects the customary law of the Yakuts, as it did that of other native tribes. For instance, we meet reckoning in Russian roubles in respect to the fines imposed for personal insults and offences (C. of Yak., XV, 1). The special significance of third thefts was similar to that in Russian law (C. of Yak., XV, 4). There were also other cases, such as the special position of individual haymow plots and the permission to rent them out (*Ibid.*, XI,)[70] etc.

Fundamental Features of Yakut Customary Law.

The Yakuts were a people of patriarchal clan culture. The basis of their clan organization was descent through the father (Usa, or Aga Usa). Seroshevsky states that until quite recently the Yakuts used the expression Yie Usa (descent through the mother). Altogether there were more than 70 Yakut clans.[71] At the head of the clan stood the clan elder. Several clans comprised a Nasleg which was called by the name of the senior clan. This unit was headed by a prince. Of several Naslegs an Ooloos was formed, its chief or head being elected from the lines of princes and elders, preference being given to the senior line. Meetings (conferences) were held of the clans, Naslegs and Oolooses. These meetings considered community business and litigations. Until recently marriages between members of the paternal clan were absolutely forbidden and complete exogamy existed. More lately this prohibition was limited to eight degrees or generations. Clan festivals were celebrated and until re-

70 The rent of haymows is called "Kortoma"—Russian expression for it.

71 At the beginning of the nineteenth century there were in the Yakut region 7 Oolooses comprising 105 Naslegs.

cently vestiges of the totemism could still be observed. In the sphere of land utilization, the haymows were divided by the clans.

The chief means of existence among the Yakuts were cattle-breeding, hunting and fishing.

The Yakuts did not know the right of private property in immovables. Immovable property pertained to the clan unions, Oolooses and Naslegs which determined its use for purposes of cattle-breeding and hunting. Pastures were divided into those used in winter and summer. There existed a special system of apportioning land for haymows by Naslegs and within the Naslegs by individual lots, due regard being given to ancestral possession, so that the same lots passed from father to son, etc., preserving the same proportions as at the time of the possessor's ancestors. Re-apportionment of haymows was permitted in the case of increase of the population or the flooding of part of the haymow land. Possessors of haymows could rent or mortgage them for a period not exceeding four years.

Juridical transactions were somewhat more fully developed than among the Tunguses. A special transaction existed—the giving of cattle for pasturing (boarding). Loans with interest were practised, the interest often being paid in kind (firewood, butter, etc.).

Polygamy existed and the power of the father, the head of the family, was very great. Marriages took place after the payment of Kalim by the bridegroom to the parents of the bride. Divorce was simple. A husband could divorce his wife for disorderly conduct or simply out of dislike for her. A husband leaving his wife without sufficient cause could not demand the return of his Kalim but was, on the contrary, obliged to return the dowry to his wife. The same position obtained with respect to divorces resulting from cruel treatment of the wife by the husband.

The heirs of a Yakut were all his children of both sexes born of all his wives (both legally wed and otherwise) taken for Kalim, but married sons and daughters had no share in the inheritance if any of the children were still single. The widow received a quarter share of her husband's property, and the husband could, if he wished, will to her all property acquired by his own labour but not that which he himself inherited. In the absence of direct descendants the heirs were the brothers and nephews.

The more complex crimes were judged by the Russian State courts. First theft of cattle was punished by payment fourfold for what was stolen, and in second and third thefts this penalty was accompanied by flogging. Fourth theft was punished by exile for settlement in Okhotsk or Kamchatka. For the theft of money or things their value was paid, the owner's losses were compensated for, and the thief was flogged. Here, too, the fourth theft was punished by exile.

For insults by word and act, dishonour (a fine) was paid, its proportions depending upon the social position of the insulted. If a clan elder was insulted and refused to accept the fine the offender was punished by flogging.

The courts were connected with the clan organization and had three or even four instances: the clan elder, Nasleg prince, Ooloos head, and Russian administrative department.

8. CODE OF STEPPE LAWS OF THE NOMADIC TRIBES OF EASTERN SIBERIA

General Information

"Code of Steppe Laws of the Nomadic Tribes of Eastern Siberia" (Draft published by the Chancery of State, 1841) pursued extensive aims — the codification of the customary law of the nomadic tribes of Eastern Siberia. Although the aforesaid Draft did not receive legislative sanction and, consequently, did not become law, nevertheless it received wide application in practice, in particular among the Buriat tribes of Siberia, until the recent times.

The appearance of this interesting record coincides with the epoch of the governmental activity of Count M. M. Speransky. Being the Governor-General of Siberia, Count Speransky in practice acquainted himself with the defects in the administration and the Courts of the native population of Siberia and made it his object to reform the said administration and Court. Due to his energy, the "Regulations Regarding the Administration of Siberian Natives" received legislative confirmation in 1822, which introduced a certain amount of definiteness and order into that sphere and for a whole century served as the basis on which the native tribes of Siberia were governed. Simultaneously, M. M. Speransky took steps towards the codification of the customary law of the native tribes of Siberia and for the creation for them of a Code of material (and procedural) law.

For the realization of the above aim, the local authorities were instructed to collect the data relative to the customs of the native population of Siberia. For the examination and the re-working of the materials collected in this manner, four commissions were established: two for Eastern Siberia — in Irkutsk and Krasnoyarsk, and two for Western Siberia — in Omsk and Tobolsk. In 1824 the commission which worked in Irkutsk compiled a Draft of the Code of Laws for the native population of the Irkutsk province, and the commission which worked in Krasnoyarsk did the same for the native population of the Yeniseisk province. Through the highest local authorities these Drafts were submitted to a special Siberian Committee, established in St. Petersburg for the Siberian affairs, of which M. M. Speransky was an active member. To the same Siberian Committee were submitted the materials relative to Western Siberia. The Siberian Committee transferred the question to a special commission, which, in 1831, compiled a draft of the Code of Steppe Laws for the Native Tribes of Eastern Siberia. This draft was again re-worked in 1836 — apparently in connection with the General Russian Code of Laws which just came into force (1832), and was printed in 1841. The Draft did not receive legislative confirmation, but, notwithstanding this, had its own interesting fate.

The need in the systematization of the customary laws of the native tribes of Siberia was so great that the draft became active law even without legislative sanction. Subsequent legislation referred to this Draft and recommended its use in deciding the cases of natives (cf. Art. 845, vol. IX, Code of laws). It was applied in judicial practice relative to the native tribes of Eastern Siberia; moreover not only by the native courts but by the government courts as well. That this Code was applied at least among the Buriats, formerly and even until the most recent times, the author has quite exact data. In particular, in 1918, the Buriat National Assembly created a National Buriat Court by way of Hoshun Courts (1st. Instance) and Aimak Courts (2nd. Instance) which acted on the basis of a special statute (Novel No. 3.) and special rules of judicial procedure. By virtue of Art. 38 of the Novel and Art. 65 of the rules concerning judicial procedure, the application of the Code of Steppe Laws was confirmed as of a Code of acting Law. The author has personally seen the resolution of the conference of Buriat judges in 1918 who recommended to each of the Hoshun Courts to have a copy of the Code of Steppe Laws for guidance. The Code was translated into the Mongol language for practical application among the Buriats. Among the latter it was distributed in manuscripts in the Mongol and Russian languages and was applied by the administrative bodies and the Courts.

The Code of Steppe Laws is divided into 6 parts and 35 chapters; it contains 802 Articles.

Part I — on family rights and obligations — contains 3 chapters: 1) on the marriage union, 2) on the union of parents and children, and 3) on taking children for bringing-up and on guardianship.

Part II — on the rights over property — contains 12 chapters: 1) on various kinds of property, 2) on the right of private use of public lands, 3) on the right of hunting and other occupations on public lands, 4) on the right of trading, 5) on the right over things and other movables which are found, 6) on the compensation in property for damages, 7) on the compensation in property for the bodily injuries and personal offences, 8) on the compensation in property for the seduction of a married woman or maiden, 9) on the compensation in property for the finding of stolen things, 10) on the compensation by means of special customs for personal damages and damage to property caused unpremeditatedly, 11) on the acquirement of rights over property transferred as a gift, allotment, by will and by succession, 12) on the acquirement of rights over property by means of barter (exchange) and purchase.

Part III — on contractual obligations — contains 2 chapters: 1) on marriage contracts, 2) on the breeding of cattle among the Yakuts.

Part IV — on good behaviour in camping ground — 8 chapters: 1) on the observation of public order, 2) on the protection of good morals, 3) on the protection of personal safety, 4) on preventative measures in case of illness, cattle-plague and the madness of animals, 5) on the prevention of fires, 6) on the preventative measures in hunting near inhabited places, 7) on the preventative measures for the protection of agriculture, 8) on special precautions in camps.

Part V — on fines and punishments — 5 chapters: 1) general provisions, 2) on fines and punishments for disobedience of the clan officials, 3) on fines and punishments for crimes against personal safety and the violation of civil rights, 4) on fines and punishments for the violation of good behaviour in camping grounds, 5) on fines and punishments for the non-observance of the prescribed precautionary measures in camping grounds.

Part VI — on judicial procedure — 5 chapters: 1) on the competence of Courts, 2) on extinctive prescription respecting law suits (claims), 3) on judicial rights and obligations of the native Courts, 4) on judicial procedure, 5) on the decision and the transfer of cases (appeals).

The concise content of the provisions concerning private and criminal law is as follows.

Private Law

The private law is set forth in the first three parts of the Code. Thus, almost half the Code (three parts of the six, and 361 Articles of 802) is devoted to private law.

Family Law. Let us examine the basic principles of the Family Law as set forth in this Code.

Marriage. Marriages of persons of native origin who embrace the Greco-Russian religion are performed according to the rites of the orthodox church. Persons of native origin who have several wives, upon embracing Christianity are compelled to select one of them for marital cohabitation and to send the others back to their relatives or to take care of them in their own clan, but the marriage with them is annulled. The wife of a non-Christian of native origin, upon being christened can cohabit with her husband if the latter obliges himself to bring up the children in the orthodox faith and to live with the wife in monogamy, otherwise the marriage is annulled (Arts. 1-3). Natives who are not Christians are allowed to marry according to their laws and customs, but the following rules must be observed: the marriageable age for men is 16 and 14 for women, before which age marriages are prohibited; it is not allowed to marry an insane or a madman, it is prohibited to marry without the consent of parents, elder relatives, guardians or mentors (*vospitateli*) (8-11). It is prohibited to compel to marry (13). Polyandry is prohibited but polygamy is allowed, subject to the following restrictions: for the Hori, Selenga and Barguzin Buriats and also for the Nerchinsk Tunguses, it is allowed for the husband, with the consent of the first wife, to take a second wife, provided the first wife during six years of marriage has no children or bears only girls; if during six years the second wife also has no children, or bears only daughters, it is allowed, with the consent of both the wives, to take a third wife, but it is not allowed to have more than three wives. If, however, the first wife bears a son but due to family or other serious reasons it is necessary to take a second wife, then the clan administration and the nearest relatives of the husband must discuss this question and the administration shall have the right to decide either to allow or to prohibit the new marriage (14). Marriages are prohibited in the following degrees of relationship: 1) between relatives along the direct (ascending and descending) line, 2) between brothers and sisters by blood, 3) between the father-in-law and the daughter-in-law, 4) between the step-son and the step-mother, 5) between the elder brother and the widow of the young brother; moreover, among the Hori and Selenga Buriats: 6) between cousins, 7) between nephews and an aunt by blood, and 8) between an uncle and a niece by blood (15).

Art. 12 is characteristic: "The abduction and the carrying-off of the daughter for the purpose of marrying her without the consent of her parents, makes the offender liable to the punishment provided for in Art. 349, and a maiden who marries independently is liable to the punishment stipulated for the insult of parents" (Art. 556). The aforesaid Art. 349 places on the offender-husband the obligation to pay a small kalim according to mutual consent, "but in no case more than 8 heads of cattle", and to return everything that the wife brought from the parental home, with the exception of her clothes and ornaments. If the husband is unable to pay the kalim, he is obliged to work for the wife's parents for a determined period, but not longer than one year.

This punishment is very light; to be more exact there is no punishment at all, because the payment of kalim is a normal phenomenon, but this provision is in accordance with customs.[72]

A marriage contract or agreement must be drawn up between the sides and submitted to the clan administration. The latter, after ascertaining that there is no compulsion, prohibited degrees of relationship or other obstacles to marriage, confirms the marriage contract and allows the marriage to be performed, otherwise the administration prohibits the marriage; a marriage entered into without the knowledge of the clan administration is considered invalid (17-20);

72 *cf.* Art. 41 Mongol Oirat Regulations, 1640; Arts. 482-4, Mongol Regulations (Code), 1815, etc.

the certificate of the clan administration, side by side with the necessary written agreement, are the chief proofs that a marriage has been entered into (21).

At the time of the engagement the bridegroom's side deposits to the bride's father or relatives a determined quantity of property which is called a "kalim" and which is designated for providing the bride with clothes, ornaments, yurt and other household necessities (328). The marriage clauses relative to the kalim of the bridegroom and the dowery of the bride are submitted to the clan administration and are entered into a book wherein such facts are recorded. The marriage contract contains the following particulars: 1) the names and surnames of those making the contract, 2) of the bridegroom and the bride, 3) the ages of the latter, 4) the time fixed for performing the marriage, 5) the contents of the kalim — the amount of money, or the quantity and the price of cattle, goods or other property, 6) the contents of the dowery and the property of the bride, 7) if the marriage is effected for exchange or without a kalim, then special conditions must be set forth — regarding the extra gifts, etc., 8) regarding a penalty, if such penalty has been agreed upon (329). It is prohibited to betroth a maiden when she is a minor and to conclude an agreement in respect to kalim or to make arrangements earlier than one year before the actual marriage. Among the natives who are non-Christians the completion of the marriage ceremony is considered the payment of the kalim in full and the taking of the bride to the bridegroom's home (330, 331).

If the bride rejects the bridegroom without a justifiable cause or marries another, and the bridegroom refuses to take another instead of the first from the same family, he must be given: 1) all his kalim back, with the off-springs thereof, and if money — with interest, 2) payment for the customary expenses connected with the match-making, 3) a quarter of the kalim which has been paid in advance, and 4) a horse or an ox must be given to the common property of the clan. If, however, the bride rejects the bridegroom for a justifiable cause, the kalim in cattle is returned without the offsprings, the money without interest, and the customary expenses for the match-making are paid with the deduction of the presents. In his turn, if the bridegroom rejects the bride without justifiable cause, he loses half the kalim and pays the aforesaid fine in favour of the clan. If the bridegroom rejects the bride for a justifiable cause, he shall be entitled to the return of the kalim in full without the offsprings (333,334).

The following are considered justifiable causes for the rejection of the bridegroom or bride: 1) mutual consent, 2) an illness which continues for more than a year, 3) madness or mental weakness, duly ascertained, 4) an evident or proved fornication or adultery, and 5) in general such crimes or offences which the natives consider as intolerable in the clan, and vicious (335). The death of the bride or the bridegroom is also considered a justifiable cause (336,337).

The Code also permits bethrothal for exchange. A person who betrothed a daughter or a female relative (for exchange) and who violates the agreement by marrying her to another is responsible for the damages suffered by the injured party and has to be fined a horse or an ox. In case when one of the sides carries out the agreement and the other side refuses to give the daughter or the female relative in exchange, the latter side has to pay 16 heads of various cattle — half big cattle and half small cattle. If one of the sides performs the agreement and the bride of the other side dies, the first side shall be paid 10 heads of cattle — an equal quantity of big and small. If one of the brides dies and the other side has not as yet given their bride to the family of the first, then the agreement is annulled without any compensation (343-344). The Code also allows marriages by working for the bride. If a poor bridegroom enters the family of the father or the relatives of the bride in order to earn the kalim and the contract which has been submitted to the clan administration relative to this has been duly carried out, and the bride refuses to marry him, or marries another, the bridegroom shall receive payment for his work according to agreement, plus 2 heads of big cattle and 3 heads of small cattle. But if such bridegroom himself rejects the bride, he shall receive only half payment for his work (347,348).

The Code of Steppe Laws also mentions dowery. "The allotment of the daughters and female relatives on account of marriage shall be effected by providing them with a dowery" (Art. 259). Brothers can not touch the dowery or other property of the sisters which has been alloted by the parents upon marriage (262). Among the tribes where there is a custom to take the kalim from the bridegroom in cattle, the dowery is considered that part of the property which the bride brings into the house of the bridegroom and which exceeds the kalim (263).

The Personal and Property Relations of the Husband and wife. — The wife who belongs to a lower estate acquires the privileges connected with the estate, rank and position of the husband. The wife is obliged to obey her husband as the head of the family, and husband and wife are obliged to live together. The property relations are separate: each of the spouse has the right to possess and acquire things into personal ownership. In particular the following are considered the separate property of the wife: clothes, ornaments, money, cattle and other movables presented to her before marriage as dowery or which came to her as inheritance, gift or by virtue of some other juristic act. The husband and wife are permitted to dispose of their property in their own name, independently of each other and without asking permission or authorization from each other. (53-63).

The Termination of Marriage. — Marriage is terminated by the death of either the husband or wife, and is annulled: by exile with or without compulsory labour for crimes (provided the wife or wives do not follow their husband into exile), by the expulsion forever from the clan by virtue of a general decision of the community of clansmen, by absence without news (during a period of 3 years) and by divorce. The legal grounds for divorce are: 1) mutual consent to such divorce, 2) the cruelty of the husband, 3) the leaving of the wife without care or the means of existence, 4) the physical incapacity to cohabit of one of the spouse, 5) the sterility of the wife, 6) evident or proved adultery (34). Divorces are effected by the clan administration (30). If the divorce is effected due to the fault of the husband, he loses the kalim and is obliged to return the dowery and the property of the wife (43). When the property of the wife has been spent with her consent the husband pays half of it upon divorce, otherwise he pays it in full (45). The wife who is divorced from her husband for arbitrarily deserting him without a justifiable cause is returned with her dowery to her father or relatives, who return the kalim, with the deduction of the marriage expenses, which must not exceed 1/3 of the kalim (46,49). A widow enjoys full liberty to contract a new marriage, while neither her relatives nor the relatives of her husband can demand a kalim in their favour; the same is the position of the wife who is divorced on account of the fault of the husband (51).

The Code provides regulations for the status of the children in cases of divorce among the Selenga and Hori Buriats (52).

Parents and Children. The birth of a child should be notified immediately. Children born in legal wedlock, as well as after the termination of the marriage by divorce effected during the pregnancy of the mother, are considered legal. Children born out of wedlock are illegal: they are included in the mother's family, but if the father is known, then from 7 years of age they are transferred to the father's family. By the marriage of their parents they acquire the rights of legal children (64-73). Childless natives are allowed to adopt the children of their relatives and of strangers; when there are own children, adoption is permitted only when such children are of age and with their consent. The person who adopts the child and the person who gives the child into adoption must notify the clan administation to that effect before witnesses, or make a written statement and submit it to the clan administration. The adopted child participates in the inheritance of the adopter with the same rights as a son by blood, but does not inherit if he does not live with the adopter and does not help him. If the adopted person grievously insults the adopter, or if he commits an evil deed, the adopter may punish him as though for the insult of parents, and if the adopted person does not improve, the adopter can demand the annullation of the act of adoption (74-79).

Majority is established at 18 years of age (98). But the parental authority is established for life and applies to children of both sexes and all ages (80). The parents have the right to apply to their children domestic corrective measures, without abusing such measures, and, in case these measures are of no avail, to complain to the clan authorities. Parents do not have a right over the life of their children, nor can they dispose of them (sell or make a gift of them), and cannot compel them to undertake deeds which are prohibited by law. The parental authority is terminated by natural death, exile or the permanent migration from the clan, provided the children do not follow the parents, and this authority is limited by: the reaching of majority, marriage, partition or by giving freedom to seek the means of sustenance (83-90).

The parents are obliged to provide their children with sustenance, to bring them up and educate them. During the time they are minors their parents manage their property. In the case of a personal insult, the parents have the right to take the part of their children and to bring action in accordance with law (91-95). The children are obliged to obey their parents and calmly heed their admonishments and corrective measures; they must honour the memory of their parents. The children must provide sustenance and maintenance to their poor and disabled parents; this obligation passes to the descendants of the children (96, 97). No law suits arising from personal relations are allowed to be brought by the children against their parents (82).

The parents can allot their children, and give them things at their discretion from their acquired property, while from the patrimonial property they can give them not in excess of that provided for by the Code. Persons who received their legal portion from the patrimonial property are considered as separated (255-257). If the father allots a son and marries him, the brothers have no claim over such property, even in case there would be no other property left after the father (260). Sons who have married and who were established by their parents are obliged to bring up their minor, weak and disabled brothers, and must in common establish a home for them and marry them; but the squanderers of the father's property have no right to such assistance by the brothers (261). The heirs have no right to demand the return of the property which the deceased during his life time alloted to the wife, relative or ward (264).

The Taking of Children to be Brought Up and Guardianship. Persons who give and take a child to be brought up must notify the clan authorities accordingly, and the latter supervise that under the guise of mentorship such children are not actually taken into a permanent hire of work. The mentor must pay taxes for the person who is being brought up and when the latter attains majority, the mentor must provide him with a home and in the case of female pupils — give them in marriage (99-102).

A guardianship is established by the clan administration over minors, the mad and the insanes. The guardians are appointed by the clan administration. The supervisory organs are the clan administration. The organization of the guadianship and its competence under the Steppe Code is in general analogous to the similar provisions of the old Russian legislation (Part I, Vol. X, Civ. Code).

Rights Over Things. The Code divides property (things) into immovables and movables. By immovables it understands the land, appendages of landed property, and permanent structures on land, such as: houses, immovable yurts and all kinds of living quarters or structures pertaining to the settled mode of life (cattle-sheds, warehouses, granaries, etc.). Movables are: movable yurts, cattle, horses, harvested and threshed wheat, all kinds of hides, furs and goods, money, monetary engagements, agricultural tools, fishing and hunting gear, burhans (idols), household implements, ornaments, clothes, food and other household necessaries. In its turn, immovables are divided into the patrimonial property (which came down by inheritance with the right of ownership by succession), and acquired property (i.e. all the other, which came by gift, will, purchase, etc.) (134-137).

In addition to the aforesaid properties of private ownership, the Code distinguishes properties which belong to institutions (property of churches and heathen temples, as well as property lent for use to persons holding offices in the Steppe administration) and public properties. To public properties the Code applies lands and appendages of landed property given into the possession of the native nomadic tribes. (138-140).

Rights Over Immovables. A part of the public land is designated as common pasture; the other land, suitable for haymows, tillage, farmsteads or camps is distributed by the community among the clansmen into lots in accordance with the number of the males from 18 to 50 years of age; this distribution is based on the locality, convenience and the area of the land. Each family enjoys its appendage of landed property by succession (141-143). For the fertilization and the irrigation of the plots, the clan administration, permits to conduct water from rivers and lakes to the plots, by means of canals, subject to the following conditions: 1) that the canals and the embankments should not prevent others from using the water, 2) that when releasing the water, others should not suffer inconvenience, and that turns should be observed, and 3) that certain places should be established through the canals to enable horses and cattle to pass over them (144), and also that the water must be conducted from such places which do not feel an insufficiency of it (155).

It is prohibited to withold by means of a dam the water at the top of such rivers or springs which are used by the nomads along its current (154). If someone, by constructing a mill or a conduit floods the above-lying mills or lands, such person is obliged to release the water and to compensate the damages (193). It is prohibited to camp or to establish any structure on the land of another without the permission of the master. With the permission of the authorities the possessor of a haymow or other land is allowed to lease them (145, 147)). On lands, which from ancient times are the common inherited property of several clans, each clan or ooloos can occupy free spaces for camping ground or pastures — until a general delimitation; it is also not prohibited for separate families to camp from one unoccupied lot to another (148, 149).

The nomadic native tribes have the right to engage in agriculture, cattle-breeding and local occupations on the waters and lands apportioned to each clan (Art. 751, Vol. IX, Old Russ. Code of Laws, *cf.* Art. 156 Code of Steppe Laws). The Russians are strictly prohibited from arbitrarily settling on the lands apportioned to the nomadic tribes; the Russians can lease land from the native tribesmen on the conditions agreed upon with their associations (*ibid.* Arts. 755, 754).

Movables. The right of ownership over movables is acquired by means of hunting, fishing, trapping, finding, and seizure of the offsprings (fruits).

The one who catches or kills a wild beast, bird or fish, acquires it into legal ownership, says Art. 159 of the Code. But the one who catches or kills a wounded or chased beast, acquires the right of ownership over it only in case if the previous hunter discontinued the chase or completely lost the beast from sight (160). Among the Southern Buriats the right of common ownership by two hunters over a beast discovered or overtaken simultaneously, is determined by means of the special customs. (*cf.* Art. 161).

It is necessary to notify the authorities regarding any found property and estray cattle. When the value of the find exceeds Roubles 7.50, or the found or lost cattle is big, the native bureau must notify the clan administrations as well as the neighbouring native bureau or district committee for the purpose of notifying the population; in case the property lost or found is considerable it is necessary to notify the general local court for the purpose of making a publication. If the owner of the lost property appears and presents the necessary proofs the lost property is returned to him against payment of 1/3 of its value to the finder, and if the lost property is cattle — payment must be made for the fodder consumed and for keeping (166-168). If within a period of two years from the notification the owner does not appear, the find devolves to the finder (174). The person who discovers a concealed find is given 1/10 of the value (or quantity) of the find (169). If someone finds an animal killed by a wild beast, or cattle which is drowned or generally destroyed, he must notify the fact and if within 3 days (7 days in winter) the owner is not found, the finder can take the hide and use the meat for food; if the cause of death is unknown, the finder must burn the animal or bury it in the ground — otherwise he becomes responsible under Art. 594 (173).

Possession. The Code regulates illegal, arbitrary possession of movable and immovable property and possession on a legal basis, and distinguishes in different ways the legal consequences of the one and the other. The person who illegally takes possession of the property of another is obliged to return it to its legal possessor and to compensate the damages arising from such illegal possession (176, *cf.* 180). If someone possesses an estate not arbitrarily but by succession, deed of purchase or by virtue of having received it from an official institution, and such person builds some structures or introduces improvements on the estate, etc., and subsequently the estate is alienated to another, the expenses for all the improvements, at the valuation of the Court, must be reimbursed to the former possessor (177). Compensation must be made for all illegal use of the property of another or for damage done to the same (180). Grass which is arbitrarily mowed on the plot of another must be returned to the possessor; among the Hori Buriats, the person who thus mows the grass must be compensated for the food consumed by him during the mowing (185). If something is sown on the land of another, it belongs to the master of the land (186).

Law of Obligations. Liability for damages. The Code of Steppe Laws lays the principle of fault in the basis of liability for damage caused. Any illegal use of the property of another, as well as damage caused to it, must be compensated (Art. 180). "Damage or loss caused quite fortuitously, or by children who have not reached 10 years of age, is not subject to compensation" stipulates Par. 4 Art. 180. "If the damage or destruction of the property of another is effected intentionally, or arises as a consequence of the non-observance of the prescribed precautionary measures, the offender, in addition to paying compensation, must be punished" (Art. 180, Par. 2). "For damage or loss caused by imprudence or ignorance, the offender only compensates the damage caused; among the Hori Buriats, however, he pays half the damages" (*ibid,* Par. 3). Thus the wrongful causing of damage carries civil liability with it; however, the accidental causing of damage, or without the possibility of imputing it to any determined person, is not subject to compensation, while the intentional causing of damage increases the liability, and the ignorant causing of damage decreases it.

However, in addition to the aforesaid general principles, the Code of Steppe Laws contains a number of concrete norms and allows a number of separate instances for the compensation of damage caused.

Thus for the prohibited fishing or hunting in the forests, lands and lakes of another, half the catch is taken away or half its value is taken into the public revenue (181). The one who steals a beast from the trap of another, or takes the fish from the nets of another, is obliged to compensate the damages, in addition to bearing the ordinary punishment for theft (183).

In case the person who trains or tames an untamed horse or ox, suffers bodily injury, then, according to the customs of the Selenga Buriats and Nerchinsk Tunguses, the expenses for curing are paid by the owner of the cattle (229). According to the customs of the Hori and Selenga Buriats as well as the Nerchinsk Tunguses a person who takes the animal of another into his herd is obliged to pay half its value in case it is lost, but if such animal leaves followed by an animal of the owner, and both are lost, no compensation is paid (230).

If a pedestrian asks a person who is riding on a horse or a cart to sit with him, and in consequence of this joint travelling the owner of the horse or cart is wounded by the sharp weapons which he has with him, or some other damage results, then, according to the customs of the Hori Buriats and Nerchinsk Tunguses, the pedestrian is obliged to pay 2/3 of the damages, and, in case of death, to pay 1/3 for the prayers to be said for the soul of the deceased. If, however, damage results to the pedestrian, the owner of the horse is obliged to compensate half the damage only in case such owner himself invited the pedestrian to ride with him (235), etc.

Contracts. The Code knows contracts relative to sale and purchase, barter (exchange), personal hire of services, hire of property, loan, forwarding, hire of work, supply, agency and partnership, but contains only brief references relative to them. The Code carries more detailed provisions relative to the marriage contract and the breeding of cattle among the Yakuts.

The Code of Steppe Laws applies gifts not to contracts but to the means of acquiring rights over property (together with the allotment, will and inheritance, *v.* Part. II, Chapter XI).

The Code divides gifts into conditional and unconditional ones. To the first group are applied the usual gifts made on account of relationship, friendship, generosity, benevolence, etc. The donor who makes a gift voluntarily and unconditionally cannot demand the return of the gift (238-241). A conditional gift or a gift subject to compensation among the Buriats, Yakuts and Tunguses takes place: 1) where, according to the ancient custom, the guest accepts from the host, or personally selects, some thing as a token of the concluded friendship, 2) where a person makes a gift to another (usually to a wealthy person) with the intention of receiving a gift in return. In such case the donee must make a gift in return. It is possible to file a complaint for the delay or the improper execution of the return of the gift; such complaints are examined by intermediaries selected by the sides (247-251).

Contracts relative to hire of services, loan of money and the leasing of appendages, is effected according to rules of the Siberian Regulations (324). "All other contracts and conditions — reads Art. 325 of the Code — are effected by the natives at the District Court or at the Clan Administration, while all the controversies relative to them are examined by the native Court according to the Regulations".

The Law of Succession. Succession by Will. The code of Steppe Laws knows succession by will and by law. The wills may be made by the natives either on general principles or in accordance with the provisions of the Code of Steppe Laws (273). These provisions are the following: According to Art. 266 of the Code, a last will, and all designations of property *mortis causa*, oral or written, must be submitted to the Clan Administration or the Native Council by the testator himself in the presence of at least two witnesses. If due to sickness the testator is unable to appear at the Clan Administration, a will made by him at home in the presence of the Clan Elder or a member of the Native Council and witnesses, is valid (267).

Last wills can be made only by persons with disposing capacity. Therefore, the wills made by persons who have not reached 18 years of age (minors), persons deprived of all civil rights by an order of the Court, insanes and lunatics, as well as suicides, are invalid (269-272).

It is allowed to leave one's property by will to relatives or strangers, subject to the following restrictions: it is prohibited to leave the patrimonial property to a strange clan or to lamaist temples without providing for the children and the nearest relatives. A widow among the Buriats and Tunguses can not transfer to a strange clan any property left to her by her husband with the exception of her dowery and her legal portion in accordance with Art. 299. Staff Lamas and bandis from the property acquired by them before entering the Order, during the life-time of their legal heirs, cannot leave more than half the property in favour of the temples, and other lamas and ubashis not more than 1/6 of the property acquired by them while holding an ecclesiastic office (265).

Succession by Law. The right to inherit is determined by the lines and degrees of relationship with the right of representation by the descending relatives. Primarily, the inheritance devolves to the descending lines, after the termination of the descending lines into the collateral lines: among the Buriats, Tunguses and Yakuts to the 4th generation. Hence the inheritance devolves, first of all, to the legal and adopted children of both sexes, and if there are no such children living — to the grandchildren and other descending relatives. If there are no descending relatives, the inheritance devolves to the first collateral line, i.e. to the brothers of the deceased and their descendants, and when there are none of these — to the second line — to the uncles and their descendants, cousins, etc. (282-286).

Unmarried daughter or daughters, in case there are brother or brothers, receive altogether a quarter, but if there are three or more sons the inheritance is divided equally among all the children (291-292).

Sons, who were separated, or who were established by means of the father's capital and married, as well as married daughters when there are unmarried brothers and sisters, do not participate in the inheritance. If there are no descendants of the male sex, the unmarried daughters succeed, but when they get married a third of the inheritance devolves to the nearest collateral relatives or the community (293-294). Step children inherit only after their own parents (297).

The parents, in accordance with the norms of Old Russian Code of Laws, vol. X, Part I, receive back after the death of their children who died without descendants, the property which was provided to them by such parents "like a gift" and the right to the possession for life of the children's acquired property (287-288).

A widow, who remained with minor children, is provided — until the sons come of age or the daughters are given in marriage — with the possession of the plot of land which was given into the use of the husband, subject to the obligation of paying the taxes and levies. When the widow gets married she loses the aforesaid right and the plot of land devolves to the heirs of the husband (277, 278). But to the widow is returned her dowry and the portion due to her from the property of the husband (the same arrangement if she does not wish to live with the children — Art. 299, Par. 4). A childless widow possesses and uses for life the property of her deceased husband, without the right of alienating it or migrating to another clan. If such widow does not wish to remain in the family of her deceased husband or marries a stranger, she is given the following part of the husband's property which is due to a widow; the dowry, clothing and ornaments which she brought with her are returned, and if she had no property, then the heirs of the husband are obliged to give her one horse with a saddle, winter and summer clothing and burkhan (Art. 299, Pars. 1-3). Upon the partition of the inheritance among the heirs, the widow or widows are generally given a fourth part of the movables of the deceased (Art. 299, Pars. 5 and 6).

The widow of a son, who owned capital in common with the parents, upon their death receives from their property 1/4 of the sum which would be due to her husband upon partition. Upon the marriage of the separate widows or upon their departing to another clan, they are given into ownership 1/4 of the inheritance which they received after their husband, while the remainder goes to the legal heirs or to the community (*ibid.* Pars. 7, 8).

The dowry and all the other property of the wife after her death, provided she made no designations in her last will, devolve as inheritance to her children, and if there were no children — either to the husband or his heirs; the relatives of the deceased wife have no right to demand such property (*ibid* Par. 11). A widow who has no children, relatives or her own property, is maintained by the relatives of the husband or the husband's clan (*ibid* Par. 12).

Escheat Property. After the death of an intestate native, who is not survived by a wife or relatives who could inherit after him, the inheritance devolves to the community property of the clan to which he belonged (301). Equally so, does the property of an intestate widow who is not survived by heirs, devolves to the property of her husband's clan (302).

The Right to an Opened Succession and the Responsibility of the Heirs. The right to an opened succession belongs to the heirs from the date of death of the testator. The heirs have the right either to accept or reject the inheritance. The person who accepts the inheritance is responsible for the debts and obligations of the testator without a limit, i.e. not only with the inherited but also with his own property (312-316).

The general period of prescription applicable to claims concerning inheritances is 10 years (*v.* 648-653).

Criminal Law[73]

General Principles. The Code divides crimes among the nomadic native tribes of Eastern Siberia into two categories: 1) those subject to criminal punishment, and 2) corrective punishments. The first are the more serious crimes which are examined in the general (Russian) Courts and are subject to punishment in accordance with the State criminal law. The second are the less important crimes and offences. They are examined in the Native Courts and are subject to (corrective) punishments provided for by the Code of Steppe Laws. But offences committed by natives outside their camps, as well as the offences of the highest official personages of native origin, when the punishment for such offences is the keeping under guard or corporal punishment, are examined by the General (Russian) Court (459, 461).

To the first category the Code applies: 1) thefts from churches and temples and the disinterment of graves for the purpose of stealing things and bodies, 2) mutiny, 3) resistance to the lawful authorities, 4) murder, 5) the inflicting of grave wounds or mutilations which endanger life, 6) the beating of a pregnant woman who, consequently, gives birth before time, 7) robbery and plunder, 8) the rape of a woman, the forceable seduction of a maid, sodomy coupled with force, 9) the making of counterfeit coins, 10) the stealing of State or public property, 11) illicit trade in wine, 12) intentional arson, 13) false accusations of crimes provided for by Pars. 1, 2, 4, 7-10 and 12 of this Article (460). All other crimes and offences are subject to the jurisdiction of the Native Court.

73 Criminal Law is contained in the fifth part of the Code.

The System of Punishments. The Native Court inflicts the following kinds of punishments: 1) reprimand in the presence of the Court or the People's Assembly, 2) fines in money, 3) the keeping under guard or temporary imprisonment, 4) labour, 5) the deprivation of a good name or public confidence, 6) corporal punishment, 7) deportation from the clan, 8) temporary suspension from office in the Steppe Administration, the deprivation of an honorary title or an ecclesiastic rank (among the Lamaists), as well as of the insignia of rank and the right to be exempted from corporal punishments (462).

The Code knows aggravating and mitigating circumstances.

Thus the punishment is increased if the offence is committed in a drunken state and the intention to commit it is proved; the instigator or the chief offender is punished more severely; the more important the inflicted damage, the severer is the punishment; the punishment is increased to those who have committed two or more offences within a short period of time or who have been guilty of several different offences (500-503).

The punishment is mitigated if the offence is committed due to ignorance, stupidity or light-mindedness; or if the offence is committed due to extreme need or poverty; or if it is committed in a drunken state without premeditation or intention; also in case of a voluntary confession and in case of a frank repentance — provided the previous conduct was irreproachable (504-508). Small children and minors (to 15 years of age) are exempted from punishment handed down by the clan courts (and must be punished by the parents); old people over 70 years of age and pregnant women are exempted from corporal punishment and are kept under arrest for a short time (509-510).

An accidental offence, committed in the course of compulsory self-defence (necessary self-defence) is not punishable; madmen and insanes are not punished; natives who embrace Christianity are exempted from punishment for minor thefts, quarrels, fights etc. (512, 515). Offences which are not discovered within ten years, or if the guilty person is not found within that time are cancelled (519). In cases of thefts within the family, the forgiveness by the head of the family or the injured party terminates judicial procedure and punishment (520). In case an innocent party is punished, he is re-established in his rights, and the judge, in addition to bearing punishment according to the service rules, is fined in favour of the injured party (521).

Let us examine the crimes and offences provided for by the Code of Steppe Laws.

Crimes and Offences Against the Administrative Order. Here are applied the disobedience to the clan officials and insubordination. Thus a person who, without good cause, does not appear at the appointed time and place at the demand of the clan officials is punished in the following manner: first time — kept under guard from 1 to 3 days; second time — in addition he is fined, in favour of the messenger, to the extent of two copecks in silver for each verst; and the third time — an ordinary clansman is punished by 15 strokes of the lash, while a person who is exempted from corporal punishment is kept 6 days under guard and is fined double the aforesaid messenger-fee. A person who does not carry out an order of his clan officials or the police concerning public affairs which do not brook delay, in addition to corporal punishment or the keeping under guard is fined in favour of the public revenue as follows: first time — one rouble, second time — three roubles, and the third time — six roubles in silver. A person who was punished three times for disobeying the orders of the clan officials and who again refused summons, and, generally, who is evidently and obstinately disobedient to and resists the clan officials, is sent to the District Court for trial according to the general provisions of law (522-527).

Crimes and Offences against the Community. The clan officials have to supervise that peace, order and good behaviour in camps are not disturbed. In case of fights, the instigators are punished as follows: an honoured clansman — 3 roubles in silver as fine into the public revenue, and an ordinary clansman — Roubles 1.50 (607-610). A person noticed for drunkeness, and specially a habitual drunkard, is appointed for labour out of turn, and in case he does not improve, such person is placed under guard or receives corporal punishment; officials who are noticed to be drunk while in the execution of their duties, are fined 3 Roubles in silver the first time, 6 Roubles the second time, and are deprived of their office the third time. Among the Hori Buriats it is generally prohibited to drink wine up to 30 years of age; from 30 to 40 years of age it is permitted to drink moderate quantities of milk wine at weddings, while from 40 years of ago onwards, a general moderate drinking of wine is permitted; for the violation of the above, honoured clansmen and Lamas who hold office are kept under arrest for 1 day, while ordinary clansmen receive corporal punishment (611-614). Persons who submit unfounded or imaginary complaints and denunciations are considered to be slanderers and, the first time, are reprimanded before the public assembly and are fined Roubles 7.50 in silver in favour of the public revenue, moreover, they have to compensate the damages arising from such slander; a person who is found to have submitted an unfounded complaint or to have indulged in slander for the second time, is kept under guard from 3 to 7 days and the fine is doubled, and the third time — in addition to the aforesaid punishment, he is recognized as not being worthy of confidence, while the fourth time such person is treated as a violator of peace and as intolerable in the clan. The same punishment is meted out to the instigators and the compilers of slanderous petitions (602-605).

Idle vagabonds, who avoid paying taxes and indulge in begging, but who are able to work, must be used by the Native Council for public works or hired to householders on the condition that back taxes and levies must be paid for them, while incorrigible offenders must be treated as intolerable in the clan (615). Persons who are recognized as intolerable in the community or clan, by virtue of the decision of the people's assemblies and clan courts, or by the orders of provincial or district officials are deported to strange and distant clans and districts (616).

Games of chance for money, property and cattle are prohibited as well as loans "which are in excess of property", (minor expenses in accordance with custom are permitted) and the offenders are punished as follows: the first time — arrest for 1 day and fine — for honoured clansmen 3 Roubles and for ordinary clansmen Roubles 1.50 in silver; the second and following times — honoured clansmen to an arrest of three days and ordinary clansmen to corporal punishment, and the fine is doubled: the lost and pledged property is returned. A person who permitted a prohibited game of chance in his house bears the same responsibility as the participants thereof (617-619). Arbitrary departures further than a hundred versts from the camp, without the permission of the clan elder, are prohibited, and further than 500 versts, without the permission of the district police; offenders are kept under guard, subjected to public works or corporal punishment (629).

The following is prohibited and is punished by fining: the concealment or the non-notification in due time of a contagious disease among cattle, the departing with diseased cattle to a healthy pasture, the using of diseased cattle for food, the non-taking of precautionary measures by an owner against a domestic animal which goes mad, against a vicious dog or animal; the setting of the steppe on fire ("pal") without taking due care, the non-taking of the necessary precautionary measures for trapping and fishing (623-634).

Crimes against a Person. The Code divides such crimes into bodily injuries and the violation of honour.

To bodily injuries the Code applies wounds and mutilations. By wounds the Code understands wounds inflicted on the surface of the body, and blows resulting in blood and blood-red spots, and the plucking out of hair; and by mutilations — the deprivation of a limb or the rendering of such limb inactive (529, 530). The infliction of light wounds makes the offender liable, depending on the damage caused, to confinement under guard, or corporal punishment and the payment of damages —— in addition to paying "dishonour"; the same punishment is inflicted for injury resulting from fright (532-533). For beating a pregnant woman, thus causing premature birth or miscarriage, the culprit is tried in accordance with general criminal laws; the same applies to serious wounds, mutilations or blows which endanger life (536-537).

According to the Code the violation of honour expresses itself in personal insults, slander, the insult of parents, adultery, sodomy, seduction and rape.

By the term personal insult the Code understands the contempt towards the person of another with the intention of offending or insulting him, or wishing to harm him, his wife, children, workers or near ones (538). An insult is divided into three kinds: verbal, in writing, and by action. An insult out of the presence of a person is not considered an offence (540, 543). An aggravating circumstance is an insult in a place of worship, at a people's administration or Court, to official, in the presence of the authorities, at a public conference, as well as insults to parents, masters and authorities (549). In cases of mutual insults the claims thereunder are extinguished, but the sides are subjected to a fair punishment (551). For an ordinary insult, dishonour must be paid; and for a grievous insult, in addition to this, forgiveness must be begged, and the offender must be kept under guard or receive corporal punishment (553,554).

Compensation for Dishonour. — For personal insults by action, when no bodily injury results, the offenders are subjected to the payment of dishonour (200). Dishonour for personal insults by action are paid as follows: 1) to the chief clan elder, the chairman of the Steppe Duma, the chief ataman of the Buriats and Tunguses cossak regiments, the chief of Mongol-Buriat clergy Hambo-Lama — 45 Roubles in silver, and among the Selenga Buriats — 2 horses (one with a saddle and bridle) and 6 rams: 2) to the Chairman of the Steppe Duma, the Chief of the Native Council, the Assistant of the Chief Ataman and the highest Mongol-Buriat clergy — the Assistant of the Hambo-Lama, Shiretu and Tsordgi — 30 Roubles in silver, 3) to a person elected by the Native Council, the Elder of the Clan Administration, a regimental chief of a hundred, shantzoba, da-lama, etc., 15 Roubles and, among the Selenga Buriats, to the persons mentioned in Pars. 2 and 3 and to the children of the chief clan elder — 1 horse with a saddle, 1 two-year-old colt and 3 sheep, 4) to an Elder at a Fair, the assistant of a clan elder, and to a chief of a cossak fifty — Roubles 7.50 in silver; 5) to a chief of ten — 3 Roubles in silver; 6) to an ordinary native, lamas and bandis who do not hold office — the amount of the taxes and land levies for 1 year, and if they do not pay such taxes and levies — Roubles 1.50 in silver (211).

For a personal insult by word of mouth or in writing, dishonour is paid to the extent of half of that due for an insult by action, while among the Selenga Buriats the persons mentioned in Par. 1 of the preceding Article can demand for such an insult — 2 horses (one of them with a saddle) and the insult of persons mentioned in Pars. 2 and 3 — one horse with a saddle, or according to the general provisions of law (212).

To wives, unmarried daughters and sons of up to 18 years of age dishonour is paid as to husbands and fathers (otherwise among the Yakuts) (213).

The compensation for insults to persons stated in Pars. 1-3, Art. 211, is paid to local benevolent institutions; however the Lamas of the lowest ranks and commoners can recover such compensation in their own favour (214).

Slander carries with it the obligation of recognizing one's words as false and the punishment is as for a false denunciation (555). The insult of parents, (when the latter make a complaint) carries with it, in accordance with the degree of the offence, a punishment by flogging or by the lash in the presence of assembled young men, or public labour for a period not exceeding 1 year, while the separated children, in addition, have to pay double the dishonour due for an insult by action (556). Adultery committed with a married woman and the seduction of a maid — upon the complaint of the husband or father — results in punishment for the offenders as for a grievous insult, and the seducer, in addition, has to pay dishonour in favour of the husband or the father of the maid (558). A person who instigates a married woman to elope with him, or who knowingly marries an already married woman bears liability in accordance with Art. 558, and if the husband refuses to take back the offending wife, the offender is obliged to pay the husband a kalim or other expenses connected with the marriage (559). A bachelor who seduces a spinster by promising to marry her, and impregnates her, is obliged to marry her, and if he denies the promise he must confirm such denial under oath (560-563). For incest, fornication with near relatives with whom marriage is prohibited, and for sodomy, the offenders must be treated as persons intolerable in the clan (565).

Crimes against Property. According to the Code the basic kind of crime against property is theft. The Code divides thefts into two kinds: theft-fraud and ordinary theft.

To theft-fraud the Code applies ordinary fraud, as well as swindle and theft, and, in certain cases, even plunder (571). Moreover, to theft-fraud the Code also applies a number of separate offences — the using of the cattle of another for riding and working purposes, without the permission of the owner, the secret shearing of a camel of another, the hiring of services upon taking an advance from several masters, and certain others (572). The Code defines as ordinary theft the following crimes: "if someone secretly takes money or other movable property without the knowledge or consent of the owner of such money or movable property, and later conceals, sells, hides or otherwise converts it to his use". To ordinary thefts the Code also applies a number of separate offences, such as: — the concealment of property given for safe-keeping, the concealment of a find, the false declaration of insolvency instead of making payment, hunting in the hunting grounds of another, the appropriation of a beast from the trap of another or of fish from the nets of another (574).

In respect to punishment both the aforesaid kinds of thefts are divided into three kinds: 1) if the value of the stolen thing is up to 6 Roubles in silver, the punishment is 25 strokes of the rods or *knout* and work from 3 to 7 days, and for those exempted from corporal punishment an arrest from 3 to 7 days; 2) from 6 to 30 Roubles: punishment by the rods or *knout*, 25 to 50 strokes, and double the term of labour: for those exempted from corporal punishment, an arrest of 6 to 14 days and the supervision of the clan administration, and 3) over 30 Roubles in silver — 50-100 strokes, and for those exempted from corporal punishment 14 to 28 days arrest and the offender is released under a guarantee, and if he is unable to provide such guarantee he is deported to a strange clan. In case of second, third or fourth theft, the punishment is increased. Moreover, a person convicted for theft is deprived of his good name. For theft accompanied by house-breaking the punishment is as for a second theft. The same in case false tracks of stolen cattle are laid in order to throw suspicion on another. Accomplices and receivers of stolen goods bear the same liability as the thiefs: persons who knowingly buy and sell stolen property are regarded as accomplices (578-600).

Such are the general characteristic of the criminal norms of the Code.[74]

The Sources of the Code

Having examined the main contents of the Code we can draw the conclusion relative to its sources.

The chief sources of the Code of Steppe Laws is undoubtedly the customary law and the customs of the native tribes of Eastern Siberia.

Having passed through a certain filtration (the Commissions in Irkutsk and Yeniseisk, and the Siberian Committee in Petersburg) the customary law of the nomadic tribes of Siberia found, however, a very strong expression in the Code.

We draw this conclusion: 1) from the content of the Code, which represents nomadic clan-patriarchal culture, 2) from the comparison with the provisions of the separate native tribes of Eastern

74 Part IV of the Code contains regulations relative to good conduct in camps, and Part VI regarding legal procedure. We shall not dwell here on the provisions of these parts, as they had no application in practice as did the norms of material law.

Siberia (Buriats, Tunguses, etc), 3) from the application of this Code not only by Russian judges, but also by native ones. In particular we draw this conclusion not only by comparing the norms of the Code with the materials of Prof. Samokvasov, which were already subjected to a certain measure of levelling but also from comparing them with the materials published by Hangalov, and with the norms of the customary law of the Buriats which is known to us by means of manuscripts and which served for internal use, e.g. the Steppe Code of the Hori Buriats 1808, Heb, 1763 of the Hori Buriats, Heb-Toktogol, 1788 of the Selengins, and others.[75] The Code contains not only the norms common to all the native tribes of Eastern Siberia, but also very many special norms concerning the separate tribes. Special regulations for the Hori and Selenga Buriats, Nerchinsk Tunguses, Yakuts and some others are often met with in the Code. The comparison of these special regulations concerning the Buriats, Tunguses and Yakuts with the Buriat and other regulations and codes convinces us that the compilers of this Code treated the norms of the customary law very attentively. Such institutions as the permission to have three wives among the Buriats and Tunguses, kalim, the abduction of the bride, marriage by working for the bride, engagement by exchange, divorce by mutual consent, divorce due to the sterility of the wife, the strong power of the head of the house, the possession of the land by clan units, the means of acquiring the right of ownership, gifts with gifts in return, compensation for dishonour, the liability for personal insults, a number of norms concerning the law of succession and many others, strikingly emphasize the characteristics of customary law. The Code is undoubtedly based on the customary law of the native tribes of Eastern Siberia, and, especially, its private law.

The second, and important, source of the Code is the provisions of the General Russian legislation, and in particular the Civil Law, chiefly the provisions of Part I, Vol. X, of the Code of Laws. On the Code of Steppe Laws reflected not only the system of distributing the material in the latter, but also much of its contents. In examining the borrowings from Vol. X of the Code of Laws and other legislations we must say the following concerning them: these borrowings chiefly have for their aim the filling of gaps of the customary law, and considerably less often the amendment of native law. For example, the customary law of almost all the native tribes of Eastern Siberia passes by in silence the question of extinctive prescription

75 *v.* the author's "Mongol Law", 1931 Appendix (in Russ.).

and regarding succession by parents. The Code introduces here the norms of Vol. X, and does the same in respect to some contracts; or, e.g., customary law says nothing concerning the utilization of the bowels of the earth, and in the additions to the Code the relative norms of the Russian Law are introduced. Sometimes we also meet amendments in the Code of the norms of customary law. For example, a childless Buriat widow after the death of her husband can go to her relatives, to her own clan, but (according the main part of customs) she can take with her only her clothing and dowery (if it survived) and according to some customs — 1/4 of the movables. The Code, however, grants 1/4 of the husband's movables and 1/7 of his immovables to the widow (the latter in accordance with the Russian provisions) or, again the Code establishes determined norms concerning the marriage of relatives and several others.

In its basis Code preserves patriarchal clan organization and nomadic economy with the week development of civil life.

In general, it is necessary to admit that, for its times, the Code was a successful attempt at the codification of the customary law of the native tribes of Eastern Siberia, which preserved its meaning (at least among the Buriats) until the first quarter of the XXth. century.

CONCLUSION

The material which is presented in this work regarding the customary law of the various native tribes of Siberia is interesting from the view point of the history of law as well as from the view point of comparative jurisprudence, as it re-establishes before us the characteristics of a legal order long outlived, with minor exceptions, by the peoples of Europe and America but which, as yet, survived strongly among the native tribes of Asia.

This material is a general review of the customary law of the nomadic tribes of Western and Eastern Siberia: the Kirghiz, Ostyaks, Voguls and Samoyeds, the Altais and Teleuts, the Tartars, Buriats, Tunguses and Yakuts, i.e. of the native tribes with a nomadic (cattle-breeding or hunting) patriarchal clan culture.

The juristic customs of the aforesaid tribes which we have examined were codified at various times: some in the XVIIth. century (e.g. the so-called laws of Khan Tiavka), others in the XVIIIth. century (the Ancient Codes of the Buriats of 1775 and 1781, the Ancient Customs of the Tunguses), and the rest in the first half of the XIXth. century. But it must not be forgotten that the origin of these customs is considerably more ancient than their codification; some of them from time immemorial (e.g. the clan order). The contents of these customs arose under the influence of various factors.

Thus when we turn to an examination of the composition of the juristic customs of the aforesaid tribes, we have to note two kinds of norms in use among them: 1) the norms which arose by way of the inner development of the customary law of the given tribes, and 2) the norms which arose on account of external, foreign influence.

In the first it is necessary to distinguish the norms which apply to one particular tribe, e.g. to the Hori tribe among the Buriats or the Nerchinsk Tunguses, and then the norms which apply to a related group of tribes, which, for instance, are in force among the Mongol or Tungus tribes, and, finally, the norms applicable among all, or the majority of, the native tribes of Siberia which we named above.

Among the second, i.e. among the customs which arose under external influences, we can note the customs, which were created under the Russian and Mongol influences and under the influence of Buddhism and Mohammedanism.

The Russian influence is noticeable on the customs of the native tribes of Siberia (from the XVIth. century in Western Siberia, from the XVIIth. century in Eastern Siberia, and from the XVIIIth. century among the Khirgiz). The Mongol influence on the customs of the tribes which were formerly under their domination (chiefly during the XIII-XV centuries, and on certain separate tribes even later, e.g. the Buriat influence on the Tunguses, and of the Djungars on the Altais and Teleuts), the Buddhist influence on the customs of the South Buriats (from the XVIIth. century) and the Mohammedan — on the customs of the Kirghiz, Voguls and Samoyeds (from the XIV-XV centuries).

Thus the customary law of the aforesaid tribes of Siberia consists of a native foundation with a number of additions which are of a foreign character in their origin, but which, however, with the passing of time combined with the original norms and entered the general composition of the customary law of the tribes we named above.

Let us now turn to the content of the norms of the customary law of the aforesaid tribes and bring out the basic characteristics common to them all and which provide the basis for the joint examination of the law of these tribes.

The basic features which are common to the customary law of all the aforesaid Turki, Ugro-Finish, Tungus and Mongol tribes are the following:—

1/ The clan organisation which lies (or recently lay) in the basis of the social organization of all the aforesaid tribes — with the clan government and clan court, exogamy and the other institutions of clan order.

2/ The patriarchal nature of the aforesaid clan order in general and of family relations in particular — with the recognition of relationship through the father, permanent marriages, the strong power of the head of the family, the father and husband, in the family, etc.

3/ The nomadic nature of the economy with a weakly developed power of the state, the absence of the right of private property in immovables and the utilization of the latter in the interests of clan unions for the purpose of cattle-breeding and hunting and, with the weakly-developed civil life, etc.

Let us examine here the above common features and institutions of the law of the aforesaid tribes.

L. H. Morgan wrote: "the gentile organisation opens to us one of the oldest and most widely prevalent institutions of mankind. It furnished the nearly universal plan of government of ancient society, Asiatic, European, African and Australian. It was the instrumentality by means of which society was organized and held together"[76].

The clan (genus) organisation was preserved in the records of the XVII-XIX centuries of all the aforesaid tribes which we have examined.

Thus we saw that the biggest of these tribes — the Kirghiz — preserved until the XX century the division into four hordes: the Greater Horde, the Medium Horde, the Lesser Horde and the Bukeiev Horde. The Hordes were divided into generations, the generations into clans, the clans into divisions, the divisions into sections, etc. Levshin, the investigator of Kirghiz life, who lived

76 "Ancient Society", Chicago, Charles H. Kern and Co, p. 61.

among the Kirghiz in 1818-1820, says that "it is hardly possible to determine all these divisions"[77]. The government of the Kirighiz rested on clan principles: all these tribal and clan divisions were ruled by the honoured clansmen: hereditary — e.g. the Sultans, the elected — Khans, Aksakals, Beys, etc. The Court of Law was held by the honoured clansmen, the Beys. This same nature of ruling and of holding Court was preserved among the Kirghiz and by the Regulations concerning the Siberian Kirghiz, 1822, the Russian control only was strengthened and judicial administration improved.

The winter pastures of the Kirghiz were divided according to the clans. Marriages were prohibited within the "taif" — generations.[78] Among the Kirghiz until recent times there existed a blood revenge by relatives (*cf.*, for example, "The Customs of the Kirghiz" — Arts. 68, 84) and the survivals thereof in the form of the "baranta" — the driving away of cattle ("Customs of the Khirghiz", 142, 143). The clansmen participated in the payment of the "koon" (a big fine in cattle) and ransom. There also existed a clan guardianship over minors. The bride (after a kalim has been paid for her) in case of the death of the bridgroom was obliged to marry the brother or some other relative of the deceased and was considered to be betrothed to the clan, to belong to the clan (Grodekov). The levirate also existed.

The modern survivals of the clan order among the Kirghiz gave M. M. Kovalevsky, the Russian investigator of the primitive law and clan life, already in 1905 the right to write that among the Kirghiz "the clan principle is still in evidence in all its force"[79]. And, with a certain measure of degradation, the clan order of the Kirghiz existed until the present time — until the Russian Revolution of 1917 and the reforms of the Kirghiz mode of life which followed it.

Among the Mongol tribes the clan order was preserved for a very long time and among certain of them it exists even at present.

Thus the clan organization among the Buriats preserved until the XX century.

(We saw above that the) Buriats were divided into 3 tribes: Bulahats, Ekhirites and Hori, and a number of generations. The aforesaid tribes and generations were divided into clans (about 200 in all), headed by the clan officials (Shulengas, Zaisans, etc.). The

77 *v.* Levshin "A description of the Kirghiz-Kaisak Hordes and Steppes", 1832, (in Russ.) Part III, pg. 6.
78 Levshin, *op. cit.*, III, 109. Kovalevsky — "Clan Life", 1905, II, 252;
79 *Op. cit*, pg. 256.

government and the Court were placed into a connection with the clan organization. Court of the first degree was held by the clan Shulenga and the honoured clansmen; of the second degree by the Chief Taisha of the tribe. The marriages bore an exogamous character (Hangalov, Petri.[80])

Mr. Petri, the modern investigator of Buriat life, who observed their life during 1914-1916, confirms the existence of clan relations among the modern Buriats.

He has written: "The Buriat clan represents a strictly exclusive community made one by the presence of a hereditary clan elder, common territory, one Ooloos, common camp sites, common local deities, common rites and sacrifices *(Talaiga)* and many other elements which shall be discussed further. Such a community lived as one large patriarchal family, closely bound together not only by common descent and blood relationship but also by a community of material interest."[81]

The elements of clan relations among the Northern Buriats, according to the same author, were common descent and blood relationship, the presence of a Clan Elder, clan lands, clan irrigation system, clan deities and clan sacrifices (Talaiga), a clan Shaman, sacred fire, clan Kurunga (sour milk), clan honour, and clan courts. He describes a special custom of breaking bones in order to divide a clan in two[82]).

As we have seen above, the Yakuts also were divided into Clans, Naslegs and Oolooses ruled by the clan officials.

In the Customs of the Yakuts the following is said regarding clan unions:

"Several families descending from a common clan chief, included from 30 to 50, 70, 100 and more souls of the male sex, and comprise a special clan which is called by the name of the clan chief from which it descends. An Elder is placed at the head of each of such clans".

80 Hangalov — Juridical Customs among the Buriats (Article); Ethnographic Review - 1894, 2, Petri — Elements of Class Relations among the Northern Buriats, 1924.

81 "Elements of Clan Relations Among the Northern Buriates", 1924, ppg. 2 *sqq.*

82 *Ibid.*

"From several of such clans — two, three or more — a Nasleg is formed which contains in itself from 100-1000 souls of the male sex and which takes for itself the name of the clan which is the eldest in origin...... A native prince rules the Nasleg." "From several Naslegs, an Ooloos is formed which is governed by a Chief" (*v.* Customs of the Yakuts, II — 1,2,3).

Mr. Seroshevsky, the investigator of Yakut life of the end of the XIX century, states that the Yakuts only recently knew a blood revenge by clansmen which used to last for 9 generations. The Yakuts knew religious clan celebrations (khisiakhi), clan haymows, clan tamgas. Marriages bore an exogamous character. Court was held by clan elders.[83]

"The clan is also the basis of the social organization of the Tunguses", wrote prof. Kovalevsky.[84]

Tungus tribes were divided into clans, with the clan officials at the head (Shulengas, Darugas, Zaisans, Toyons and clan princes). The Court was placed in connection with the clan organization. Here existed clan haymows, clan hunting grounds and fisheries. Marriage bore an exogamous character.

We also find clan unions (suyeks) and the ancient military divisions into tochuns (forties) among the Altais and Teleuts, with the clan officials at the head (Shulengas, Zaisans). Marriage was exogamous and was not allowed within the limits of the clan union (suyek). Clan assistance existed here as well.

In the legal customs of the Voguls, Ostyaks and Samoyeds, we meet with the indications to their clan elders and native princes. The administration and the Court were in the hands of the clan elders, and the native princes (*v.* Customs of the Vogus, etc. Art. 2) under the supervision of the Russian authorities. *Cf.* also Customs of the Kusnetzk Tartars, Art. 3rd.

It is necessary to note an interesting phenomenon connected with the clan organization and the strengthening of clan solidarity: the existence, among certain tribes, side by side with the codes of punishments, of a system of rewards for the doing of certain generally-useful and also altruistic deeds to the advantage of the clan and tribe (and the separate members thereof); this system was even accompanied by punishments for not undertaking such deeds.

83 Seroshevsky, Yakuts, Vol. I, 433 sqq., *cf.* Koralevsky, Clan Life,, II, 235 sqq. (both Russ.).
84 *Ibidem.* p. 241.

This phenomenon found a strong expression among the Mongols *cf.* Mong.-Oirat Regul-s of 1640-14, 109, 108, Khalkha Djirum-XII, XV-3, etc.[85], but is also met with in the records of the Buriat and Tungus law.

Thus Buriat law prescribed a reward (one horse) for saving a man from fire or water, while a punishment (flogging) was inflicted for reluctance or neglect in aiding such a victim. Art. 11 of the ancient Code of the Horins, 1781, stated: "He who did not give aid to a perishing man was subjected to corporal punishment; while he who saved a man received a horse in reward." An analogous rule was contained in Art. 85 of the Steppe Code. "Seeing a man who has fallen victim to fire or water, do not abandon him without pulling him out and giving him your attention. Anyone seeing such a thing must give aid and pull him out. As a reward for saving the victim, a horse shall be given......And if anyone pays no attention, let him be scourged" (Steppe Code, Art. 85).

The customs of the Nerchinsk Tunguses (Art. 41)[86] contain the following regulation: "Anybody seeing anyone in fire or in water must immediately apply all his efforts and all the means at his disposal in order to free and save him. But should it be impossible to save him, then he must immediately notify the people nearby, no matter to which community they belong. Anyone who, seeing a man in such danger, makes no attempt to save him, will be beaten in accordance with "legal order".

Among all the aforesaid tribes there existed a clan court with the participation of the clan officials and the honoured clansmen.

The marriages were exogamous. This is confirmed by the investigator of Buriat life, E. B. Petri. "The Buriat clan", he writes, "is completely exogamous and no marriage can take place within the clan. In relation to any given clan all other clans fall into two groups, the 'Halu' or 'Halun' (warm, own) and 'Hari' (foreign). Marriages with the 'Halu' are forbidden. This group includes clans related territorially, and also clans bound to the given group by common descent which had not yet performed the ceremony of 'separation of the bones'. The 'Hari' group included all other clans and marriages with their members were permitted." (*ibid,* pg. 5).

85 *v.* in more detail: Riasanovsky - Fundamental Principles of Mongol Law, ppg. 224-225, 303.

86 *v.* Samokvasov, "Collection of the Customary Laws of the Siberian Natives", 1876, pg. 34.

Among the Kirghiz and the Yakuts exogamy formerly bore an absolute character, but in modern times it was somewhat modified. Thus Levshin, who observed the customs of the Kirghiz in 1818-1820, wrote that the Kirghiz "when selecting wives from their own people observe the most distant degrees of relationship",[87] and Kovalevsky in 1905 stated that marriages between Kirghiz are prohibited within the limits of the Taip and 6 degrees of relationship.[88] Seroshevsky, who lived among the Yakuts at the end of the XIXth. century wrote that marriages among the Yakuts are prohibited within the limits of 8 generations, but that "certain Yakuts directly denied that within the father's clan persons could be found with whom marriage is possible".[89] Apparently, absolute exogamy was weakened here only recently. Among the Altais and Teleuts marriages are prohibited within the limit of the clan unions (Direnkova[90]), also among the Tunguses (Shirokogoroff.)

Thus among the aforesaid nomadic tribes the clan was an union of blood relationship, a religious union (clan gods, clan festivals, etc.), an economic union (a common economy: common clan pastures, common clan haymows, hunting grounds and fisheries, common irrigation, etc.), an union of a public-legal nature performing certain functions of the State (clan officials, clan court, clan revenge, clan guardianship, clan assistance, etc.).

The clan of the aforesaid tribes had a patriarchal, agnate character. The characteristic elements of the patriarchate, of patriarchal relations are: 1) the recognition of relationship through the father, 2) the permanency of marital relations (the marriage of a determined man to one or several determined women), and 3) the power of the head of the family — the father — over the family (Jenks).

Here relationship is counted and recognized only through the father's line, i.e. only the relatives through the father enter the clan. Relationship along the mother's line is not taken into account, it is not considered as relationship (and usually is not considered an obstacle to marriage). All clan relations deal with relatives through the father. Only regarding the father's clan and respecting the relations within the limits of the father's clan (with very minor exceptions) are mentioned in the juristic records which are known

---

87 *op. cit.*, III, 109.
88 *op. cit.*, 252.
89 *op. cit.*, 435.
90 the stated article.

to us and which deal with the aforesaid tribes. The patriarchal, agnate character of the clan with the recognition of relationship only through the father is confirmed by the investigators of the life of the aforesaid tribes, e.g. Hangalov ragarding the Buriats, Seroshevsky — the Yakuts, Georgi, Shirokogoroff — the Tunguses, etc.

Moreover, in distinction to group marriage (the marriage of a certain group of men to a certain group of women), which is characterized by the absence of permanency and definitiveness in marital relations, we have, under the patriarchate, a permanent marriage of one determined man to one or several determined women.

The initial kind of such permanent marriage, which results in the individual possession of a woman, is marriage by means of abduction, the carrying off of a wife, from a strange clan. The next stage is the buying of a wife from her clansmen. And, finally, an individual marriage by means of the consent of the sides. These three chief kinds of marriage have a number of intermediary varieties.

The nomadic tribes described by us above knew the second type of marriage as basic — the purchase of the wife in a modified form, by paying ransom for the bride — the so-called "kalim".

In the "Customs of the Yakuts" it is stated: "The Yakuts get married by giving for the wife an agreed quantity of live and slaughtered cattle, and, sometimes, money, at determined time and in parts, which is called a kalim" (XIV).

In the "Customs of the Tunguses of Gantimurov", among other things it is said: "She was bought from him for a kalim" (Suplem. 5).

In the Customs of the Kuznetzk Tartars it is stated: "arrange (persuade) to give a daughter in marriage, promising to give a "kalim" — according to agreement the payment is in cattle or in money" (Art. 11).

In the "Customs" of the Balagansk and other Northern Buriats it is stated: "a wife taken by a Buriat is considered as bought but not as a serf......" (VI — Introduction). In the "Customs of the Selenguins Buriats" it is said: "if within 2 years no one will seek her in marriage......so (relatives) must sell such wife to some one who wants her and thus obtain the kalim due" (to the former husband) (Art. 56).

Side by side with marriages for a kalim there exist certain other kinds of marriages. Such, for example, is the ancient form of marriage, known in the Bible, marriage by working for the bride: when the bride-groom works for a number of years for the bride's father in lieu of paying ransom for her. This kind of marriage is known to the Buriats (*cf.* Jurid. Cust. of Hangalov,-7), Tunguses (Lichkov), Voguls, Ostyaks andSamoyeds (Cust. of Vog.-17). Among the Buriats and Tunguses there exists also a marriage by exchange: the marriage of two pairs, when the son of the first family marries the daughter of the second family and when, simultaneously, the son of the second family marries the daugher of the first family (*cf.* St. C. - 14, C. of Verkh. Bur. - 17, 19, C. of Gant. Tung. 11 and Suppl. 3).[91]

But here were also preserved the survivals of a more ancient form of marriage by means of the abduction and the carrying-off of the bride.

Thus, among the Kirghiz, after the religious ceremony according to the Moslem rites, the young wife is placed in a special kibitka, surrounded by women who sing songs. The young husband rides to the doors of the kibitka and wishes to enter, but for a long time he is prevented from doing so. Finally, he bursts in by force, takes away his wife from the women who surround her, places her next to him on the horse and takes her away with him (Levshin).

Among the modern Buriats there exists the following custom: the relatives who are taking the bride to the bride-groom pull her towards them, and the relatives who are remaining at home pull her towards them; it is only after the former have succeeded in pulling the bride over to them are they entitled to take her to the bride-groom (Potanin).

The symbolic abduction of the bride forms a part of the marriage ceremony also among the Yakuts.

The abduction of brides with their consent were met with in the XIXth and XXth centuries among the Buriats, Altais and Teleuts, also, apparently, among the Yakuts and the Tunguses.

All the aforesaid tribes permit polygamy (evidently, also, a survival of the group marriage).

We find indications regarding polygamy in the Buriat Customary Law of the Northern Buriats (The Customs of Hangalov — 6) and the Southern Buriats (The Customs of the Selenguins — 59,60),

91 We meet both forms of marriage in the "Code of Steppe Laws of the Native Tribes of Eastern Siberia," *v.* Arts. 343-344, 347-348.

in the Customs of the Yakuts (XIII), in the customs of the Kirghiz (Art. 202) and some others.

Levshin ascertained this fact in respect to the Kirghiz and states that the Khan Nuhr-Ali of the Lesser Kirghiz Horde had 16-17 wives and 15 concubines. Georgi, a learned traveller of the XVIIIth. century, wrote that the Buriats are allowed to take as many wives as they can afford to buy: four, five, two, one.

Lichkov informs regarding the existence of polygamy among the Tunguses[92].

But it is necessary to bear in mind that here polygamy is at a decline, at a stage of transition to monogamy.

Thus we see that among the Kirghiz and Mongol tribes one of the wives is distinguished as the eldest or the chief mistress of the house and the keeper of the hearth and the other wives occupy a lower, subordinate, position. This is the first step toward monogamy. The second step is the placing of the secondary wives in the position of concubines (like in China, in the epoch of the Ta-Tzin Dynasty) and, finally, the non-recognition of the juristic position of the secondary wives or concubines (as in China in the epoch of the Republic — according to the Civil Code) or a direct prohibition to have such wives.

Further we see that by means of customs special measures are being worked out to prevent the growth of polygamy.

Thus the number of wives among the Yakuts is limited to five (The Customs of the Yakuts — XIII); among the Buriats it is permitted to take a second (and third) wife only in case there is a serious reason (e.g. if there are no sons, the sickness of the wife) and with the permission of the Authorities; and it is not allowed to have more than three wives (Cus. of the Sel. 59, Cus. Han. — 6); among the Kirghiz a bigger kalim has to be paid for an extra wife than for the previous one, which prevents the development of polygamy (Levshin, III, 98).

Polygamy is rare among the modern Kirghiz (Levshin), Buriats (Petri), Tunguses (Lichkov), Altais and Teleuts (Dyrenkova.)

The power of the head of the family, the father, over the family is very great among the aforesaid tribes.

---

92 *v.* Enc. Dictionary of Brockhaus and Efron, book 67, pg. 67.

Formerly this power extended to the right of the father, and the parents in general, over the life and death of the children and subordinates, the survivals of which right are preserved in their legal customs, in particular among the Kirghiz.

Thus in the Mongol epic folk poem "Geseriad" which was recorded in writing approximately at the beginning of XVII century, we find an indication: the mother advises the husband to kill the newly-born hero Geser, but the husband does not consent.

In the old Kirghiz legal customs, the so-called laws of the Khan Tiavka, XVIIth. century, we find a rule to the effect that the parents shall not be punished for the killing of their children (Art. 5) and the masters have the right over the life and death of their slaves (15). The same provision regarding the freedom from responsibility of the parents for the killing of their children is also contained in Art. 87, Customs of the Kirghiz, codified in 1824 (*v.* also Art. 200). Equally so is there an indication in these Customs to the effect that a master bears no responsibility for killing his servant (79) and his Kalmuck slave (80).

According to the so-called laws of Khan Tiavka, if the husband kills his wife he can redeem himself by paying a property fine — a koon, but if the wife kills her husband she "shall assurely be executed" (4).

The right of the parents and the elder relatives to punish their minor children and descendents exists among all the aforesaid tribes, as does the right of the elder relatives to the honour and respect on the part of the younger relatives.

But it is necessary to note that the authority of the father and parents in general began to be considerably modified in the XIXth. and XXth. centuries. This authority was preserved the strongest among the Kirghiz (*cf.* Arts. 87, 104, 200 and 201, Customs of the Kirghiz), but here also, side by side with the authority of the father, arose the authority of the mother and, parental authority underwent a certain modification (*cf.* Art. 200, second par.).

Side by side with the sharply defined features of the patriarchate we also meet among the aforesaid tribes considerable survivals of the matriarchate.

Thus Mr. Seroshevsky points out that although relationship among the Yakuts was considered through the father, still the word "clan" is usually designated (end of XIXth. century) by the term yie-usa (yie — mother, usa — clan) but not aga-usa (aga — father) and further that many clans and naslegs of the Yakuts trace their descent to a woman.

Notwithstanding the non-recognition of relationship through the mother's line, the mother's clan occupied an honoured position — in particular the mother's brother, the maternal uncle (*avunculus*).

Thus among the Altais and the Teleuts the maternal uncle (Tai) participated most closely in all the chief events of his nephew's life, replacing the father; and his children enjoyed special honour and respect on the part of the nephew, their cousin. The maternal uncle is obliged to give presents to the nephew, which the latter is even permitted to demand through the Zaisan (Potanin, Direnkova).

Among the Mongol tribes it was considered lucky to take a wife from the mother's clan. Among the Buriats the maternal clan is called by the name of the maternal uncle — *nahsanut* — and such uncle has to patronize the nephew by the mother, and the latter has to show honour and respect to the mother's clan as well as to his wife's clan (Petri).

Among the Altais and the Teleuts there still remains an interesting survival of group marriage — the classificatory system of relationship, by virtue of which there existed special classes of relatives, say the class of brothers (by blood, cousins, cousins once removed), sisters, grandfathers, etc. All the relatives of a given class are considered to be of the same degree of relationship (Direnkova). This is a survival of the epoch when all the brothers were considered the husbands of all the sisters.

The classificatory system of relationship existed also among the Yakuts[93].

Among the Kirghiz, Buriats, Altais and Teleuts, there remained still another survival of the group marriage — the levirate, i.e. the marriage to the widow of the deceased brother. But the former compulsory nature of this marriage is modified in the present customs.

The following is said regarding this question in the Customs of the Kirghiz: — "Whoever dies childless, his wife, if he had only

93 M. M. Kovalevsky — "Clan Life", 1905, p. 154 (in Russ), *cf.* Tahtarev — "A Comparative History of the Development of Human Society and Social Forms", I, 1926, pg. 321 (in Russ).

About the classificatory system of relationship and group marriage see Morgan-"Ancient Society" 403, 412, etc. Kohler — "Zur Uhrgeschichte der Ehe", 1897, III.

one, shall go to the elder brother, but if there were two, three or more, then shall the brothers, if there are any, take one each, but only with the consent of the wife and in no case shall they be compelled by force to marry" (200).

Among the Verholensk Buriats the custom of the levirate is confirmed, but the possibility for the wife to evade it is stated (Customs of the Verkh. Buriats — 20).

Certain other survivals of the matriarchate were preserved among the aforesaid tribes (e.g. the survival of heterism among the Buriats, Tunguses, Kirghiz, the recognition of relationship along the mother's line among the Voguls, etc.).

Among the Kirghiz, Yakuts, Kuzntezk Tartars and several others there survived the interesting traces of an ancient time — totemism.

The nomadic form of life common to all the aforesaid tribes also influences their law to a considerable extent and is conductive to the creation of a number of characteristic legal phenomena. The most important of these should be considered: 1) the weak development of the government State principles, 2) the absence of the right of ownership over immovables, and 3) the insignificant development of civil life.

According to the opinion of L. H. Morgan the germs of government originate from a clan organization in the epoch of savagery[94]. But these germs were not stable and developed very slowly among the nomadic tribes.

The dispersion of the camps of the separate tribes and clans, the possibility of moving about easily and the possibility of departing to camp to distant places — all this prevented the centralization of authority and its strengthening. The clan order and nomadic culture are not a firm basis for the establishment of a strong State power, for the development of state principles. The separate nomadic tribes can quite quickly unite for the realization of some common aim (campaign, defence) or to create a State under the influence of a strong and talented leader, but with the attainment of a given aim or with the death of the leader, such unions very quickly fall apart into their original elements. Due to this, considerable nomadic states easily originated in Middle Asia (Huns, Sanbiss, Jujanes, Turks-Tugu, Uigurs, Hagas, Kidans, Manchus, Mongols, and certain

---

94 "Ancient Society", pg. 5.

others). But all these States were not long-lived and quite quickly fell apart[95].

The Empire of Jenghiz Khan, the strongest of these States, was also not long-lived; already at the time of his grandsons it fell apart into appanages which latter were further divided and disappeared. The nomadic State of the Kirghiz was also not long-lived, notwithstanding its talented rulers, such as Arslan and Tiavka.

The weakness of the State principles, notwithstanding the exceptionally extensive scope of the personal power of the chiefs and rulers, is characteristic of the nomadic tribes.

Due to the weakness of the authority of the State, naturally the judicial functions of the State were also weakly developed, and the administration of justice was also badly organized.

Thus among the Kirghiz who later than the other tribes came under the domination of Russia, and longer than the others preserved their ancient organization and the mode of life, we meet with frequent cases of permitted taking the law into one's own hands — the killing of the criminal on the scene of the crime (in the *flagrant delit*). And this position we find not only in the customs of the XVIIth. century (*cf.* Tevka, 9, 13, 15) but also in the customs of the beginning of the XIXth. century (*cf.* C. Kir. — 1, 95, 79[96]). Here we also meet the giving of criminals for trial and punishment by injured parties or their relatives according to the so-called laws of Khan Tevka (*cf.* Tevka, 1, 2, 4, 29), as well as according to the customs of the XIXth. century (*cf.* C. Kir. 84, 86, 96[97]), as well as the trial by relatives instead of by the State Court (Tevka — 5, 16; C. Kir. — 87, 96).

The organization of the courts among the Kirghiz, before they came under the domination of the Russians, was established very badly. Here the Russians found a sole Court by the Beys without the possibility of appeal, because no higher instance existed. The complaints against this Court were general. And the Statute of 1822 besides excluding the most important criminal cases from the competence of the local court and local punishments, also created a second instance over the court of the Beys.

95 Haruzin called such state formations "the clan states" — Ethnography, III, pg. 223, *et seq.*

96 Art. 95: "The one who arbitrarily kills a thief, robber or murderer, no sin shall be imputed to such a person, and it is permitted to destroy the thief, robber or murderer without compensation or rebuke."

97 Art. 84: "If one, two, three or more kill one or more persons, then to the plaintiffs one shall be given up, whom they demand, for immediate execution. . . . "

Among the other native tribes, who were earlier than the Kirghiz dominated by the Russians, the latter, after conquest, also found no correct organization of the administration of justice. The beginnings of the latter were laid by the instruction of Count Raguzinsky in 1728 (the establishment of a Court by 6 honoured clansmen, with the exclusion of the most important criminal cases from the competence of the native Court). And only by the Statute of 1822 the principles of more correct judicial organization and procedure were created here.

Of the other institutions of public law, let us note in brief the condition of the criminal law, *viz.*, the system of punishments.

In the Customs of the Kirghiz we find the principles of their old criminal law. Here, in the so-called laws of Khan Tevka of the XVIIth. century, as well as in the customs codified in 1824 we meet with a blood revenge by relatives (Tevka — 1, 2; C. Kir. — 84, 86) and severe punishments, the frequent application of the death penalty (for murder, robbery, theft, adultery, rape, the abduction of a married woman, incest, blasphemy and certain others, *cf.* Tevka, 2, 4, 8-10, 12, 13, 15; C. Kir. — 2, 3, 8, 67, 118, 127, etc., and other severe and painful punishments (*cf.* Tevka — 2, 13 and others; C. Kir — 69, 97, 113).

But we must also note the evolution in the penal system of the Kirghiz: the punishments of the XIXth. century are in general milder than the penal system of the XVIIth. century. This modification increased subsequently after the publication of the Statute of 1822, due to the change in the living conditions and the Russian influence.

We find the same phenomenon among the Buriats. In the XVIIth. century the Russians found here quite a severe penal system which included the death penalty and other severe punishments. Gradually, under the new conditions of life, this penal system grew milder, and this process was also assisted by some of the measures of the Russian authorities (*e. g.* the exclusion, in 1728, of the most important crimes from the competence of the local Courts).

We could observe the same process among the Ostyaks and Voguls, in the customs of which tribes severe punishments were preserved for certain crimes by the natives-Moslems, *e. g.* for apostasy, robbery, theft, according to the principles of the Koran and the Moslem law.

Further, the extensive nomadic economy which is necessarily conducted in common by the clan unions, demanded the presence of great spaces of land and exceptional possibilities for the individual acquirement of immovables.

T. Levshin wrote the following regarding Kirghiz economy:— "The primary and almost the exclusive source of wealth of the nomadic hordes, the primary and the most beloved of their occupations consists, as has been said above, of cattle-breeding, and for the maintenance of such cattle-breeding within extensive limits in which it is practiced at present it is necessary to have great open spaces which cannot, and should not, have exact limits." (*op. cit.*, III, 26). A. I. — describes the summer wanderings of the Kirghiz with their herds in the following manner: "Each clan or aoul, year in and year out, follows one and the same route, stopping at the same springs and wells where their ancestors stopped hundreds of years ago, and gradually returns for winter camping to one and the same place."[98]

Under the nature of steppe economy as described above, the right of ownership over immovables, is not known to the nomadic tribes, as a rule. Only with the transition to semi-settled and settled stages do we notice the signs of the development of the right of ownership over immovables, which right is connected with a special form of labour devoted to the cultivation of such immovables, with the consequent transition to the more intensive forms of economy.

Thus the Yakuts allow each clan member to clear the forests, drain the marches and lakes and in this way to establish haymows, fence-off the same and use such haymows "in remuneration of labour and damages" for a term of 10 years without the participation of the other clan members; when dividing the haymows "the antiquity of possession is respected, so that they pass from father to son, etc. in the same quantity which the ancestors possessed" (XI — 2, 3). However, here in exceptional cases a decrease of such haymows is permitted, i.e. some sort of a repartition (*ibid*). Among the Selenga Buriats a plot of land specially worked into a haymow or a tillage with water conducted thereto do not participate in a general partition (Cus. of the Sel. — 163, *cf.* also the Cus. of Verhol. Buriats 34, 40).

98 Prof. Leontovich wrote the following regarding the Western Mongols and Kalmucks: "An extensive cattle-breeding is the only economic item which to any extent provides security to the steppe cattle-breeder in the weakly producing Steppe, and this prohibits the division of the Steppe into permanent lots with the resulting destruction of the system of common use" (*op. cit*, 256-8).

Personal ownership of movables is already distinguished here from the clan family property, whenever such property was acquired by the personal labour of the owner.

According to the customs of the Horins, if anyone wounded a fox or wolf and gave chase to the wounded beast, and if the beast was slain by another hunter, the beast belonged to the first hunter and its four paws to the second. But if the first wounded a she-goat and the second killed it, the entire beast went to the second (St. C., 104). It was presumed that for a small beast the first shot was fatal, while for large game the fatal shot was the second, etc.[99]

Moreover, this ownership received its development not only in the laws of the Mongol tribes but also among the other aforesaid tribes.

Thus, for example, among the Voguls, Ostyaks, and Samoyeds, "a vitally wounded beast belongs to the one who wounded it first, while a lightly wounded beast to the one who kills it first" (The Customs of the Voguls and others, Art. 22). It is prohibited to take out a fish or a beast from the trap of another; for the second and third offence, the offender receives corporal punishment in addition to the usual punishment (*ibid.*, *cf.* Customs of the Kirghiz, 173). Among the Tunguses: "the one who first wounds a beast and chases it, while another on account of the meeting kills it, he shall take the beast who wounded it first" (Customs of the Tunguses of Gantimirov, 75, *cf.* Customs of the Yakuts — XI, I), etc. We meet analogous norms among other of the aforesaid tribes.

It is necessary to mention the still insignificant development of civil life here — which is connected with a nomadic, semi-natural economy. The chief kinds of transactions are gratuitous deals: gift, loan for consumption, loan without interest, of the non-gratuitous transactions — barter (exchange) is developed, later — loans with interest, rent and some others. In general, civil life and non-gratuitous transactions are most of all developed among the Buriats, and after the Buriats among the Kirghiz and Yakuts.

It is necessary to note the special character of the gift among the nomadic tribes, such as the Buriats, Tunguses, Yakuts and certain others, which is different from the modern contract of gift and which is the survival of the ancient community of clan property and clan hospitality (*cf.* in particular the Cust. of Yak. — XXIX, 2, 3).

99 *v.* in detail Riasanovsky — Fundamental Principles of Mongol Law. ppg. 245-6

Thus the Buriats were a very hospitable people and guests were treated with the greatest consideration. They were offered food not only by their hosts but also by the kinsmen of the latter members of the same Ooloos.[100]

Furthermore, gifts were bestowed upon the guest. The custom was that anything that pleased the guest or for which he asked was to be given him. On the other hand, custom dictated that the guest was also to make a present to the host when the latter came to return his visit. Thus "if anyone who came to another's house as a guest and offered him friendship was in need of a good trotter, a camel or any other thing, and got what he wanted, and if afterwards the giver of this gift called on the receiver and claimed a present from him which the latter refused to bestow, then, according to the customs of the Horins, the Court returned to the giver what had been taken from him, and the receiver, if he was a commoner, was in addition subjected to corporal punishment, and if he was a Sait — was fined for the profit of the people". (St. C. 123). If the gift is made without a request and the donee does not make a gift in return, then the donor has the right to demand the return of the original gift (124). But according to the Customs of Horins of 1823, whoever made a gift for friendship's sake and without being asked had no right to claim its return (C. of Hor. B., XII, 7). According to the customs of the Selenguins a gift always required a return gift, irrespective of whether it was made voluntarily or upon request, but suits arising from disputes in this connection were settled not by the Court but by honorary mediators (C. of Sel. B. 110, 112).

Among the Tunguses, as among the Buriats, gifts demanded similar gifts in return, and the return was to be equivalent in value to the original present (Cust. of Nerch. Tung. — 19). However, if the receiver of the gift had notified the donor that he could return only a trifling present, this was permitted (Cust. of Gant. Tung. —27).

In the Customs of the Yakuts it is said: "One presents to another cattle, money, things, animal hides, etc., as a sign of friendship and mutual admiration, in the hope of receiving a gift in return; the donee makes a much bigger gift in return and notifies that he will also visit the donor; in this way mutual visitations and gifts continue until the gifts of the first are equal to the gifts of the

100 *Cf.* Riasanovsky — "Customary Law of the Mongol Tribes", 1929, p. 194.

second, i.e. by equivalent gifts, gifts in return are terminated" (XXIX-2).

There were, however, gifts which did not demand return and were given without the intention of receiving any compensation.

Thus in the same "Customs" it is stated: "gifts are made which are called *tennbiat besiakh,* i.e. gifts without a gift in return, as gratitude for some favour or services — from the clan elders to the clansmen, and from the clansmen to the clan elders, as well as among equals, clan elders, clansmen, without any demand for compensation; therefore, claims concerning presents of this kind are not satisfied." (XXIX-3).

From the above it is clear that originally all gifts required an equal gift in return, otherwise the original gift had to be returned, or a compensation had to be made (St. C. 1808 — 123; C. of N. T. — 19; C. of Yak. — XIX, 2). Later, however, deviations were permitted: if the gift was made out of friendship without the request of the donee; or if the donee stated that he is poor and is unable to make an equal gift in return, it was not permitted to demand the return of the original gift (C. of H. B. — XII, 7; C. of Gant. Tung. — 27). Finally, the Yakut Law stipulated a category of gifts which were not to be compensated (XXIX-3). Only such gifts which do not require a gift in return or a compensation can be considered gifts in the modern meaning of the word, i.e. a non-gratuitous transfer of property by the donor to the donee.[101]

Thus, gradually, from the mutual clan hospitality there developed a gratuitous transfer of property — the gift in the modern sense.

Let us also note the question concerning the compensation of damages, which is of considerable importance in civil life.

Primitive law connected responsibility with the causing of damage independently of the subjective fault (*culpa*) of the author of it. Whether the person causing the damage acted with or without premeditation and evil intent, consciously or unconsciously, the very fact of the damage having been caused served as a ground for responsibility, for which reason responsibility was attached to minors,

101 Code of Steppe Laws knows two kinds of gifts: non-conditional (absolute) and conditional: the first is an ordinary gift without compensation. The second, applicable among Buriats, Tunguses and Yakuts, requires a compensation (two cases: 1) a gift to a guest, 2) a gift made with the intention of receiving a gift in return.) (Arts. 247-251).

madmen and even animals. With the development of social relations, the grounds of responsibility underwent a gradual change: from the outward objective criterion of damage, law (both criminal and civil) passed to an inward subjective view based on considerations of justice — the fault of the author in the causing of the damage. Acts which were not the result of his evil intent (*dolus*) and could not be proved to involve the fault (*culpa*) of their author, or at any rate negligence (*culpa*) came to be regarded as accidental and not involving responsibility on the part of anyone.

As a general rule modern law places responsibility in accordance with the principle of fault, but allows the application of the principle of causing in certain special cases.[102]

Native law presents a picture of transition from primitive responsibility for damages on the principle of causing (cause) to the fixing of responsibility on the principle of fault.

Thus, Buriat law passed over to the fixing of responsibility on the principle of fault. Children (under eight years old) were not answerable for damage caused by them (St. C., 70). If anyone accidentally ran against a fence, the owner of the latter was not responsible for the damage (St. C., 94). If a labourer hired out for money died of disease or was crippled through his own carelessness, the master was not responsible (C. of Sel. B., 119) etc. (*cf.* St. C.-72, 99, 129, C. of Sel. B. — 166, C. of Verh. B. — 41, 44).

However, besides these provisions fixing responsibility, on the principle of fault (*culpa*), we meet with a series of provisions of private law in which the other (old) point of view (the causing) was applied but usually with diminution of responsibility.

Thus if anyone accidentally caused damage and loss to another, the damages were borne equally by both parties (C. of Hor. B., II, 10). If anyone commissioned another to make a hilt for a knife, or a handle for an axe, and the other during his work accidentally cut himself or even died, the man who commissioned him was liable for two thirds of the expenses (St. C. 24, 25;) etc. If, during a hunt, an arrow struck another hunter, the man who shot it was obliged to make good the damage (St. C., 126).

Tungus Law, in principle, also places responsibility for damage caused in accordance with the principle of fault.

---

102 *cf.* e.g., Riasanovsky — Chinese Civil Law, 1938, ppg. 133-140.

Thus a child under 8 years of age who causes damage bears no responsibility (C. of N. T. — 25). A person who breaks or burns some thing on a strange camping ground bears responsibility for damages and is punished by beating with rods (C. of N. T. — 36). A person who dug a hole at a camping ground is obliged to fill it up, when leaving camp, otherwise he is responsible for the damage caused to the cattle of another which falls into such hole (C. of G. T. — 71).

But Tungus law, like the Buriat law, allows responsibility in accordance with the principle of causing, subject to a lesser measure of compensation. If a person requests another to sharpen an axe or a knife for him, and the latter cuts himself due to his own mistake, then the person requesting such service pays 2/3 of the damages (C. of N. T. — 12). If a person requests another to slaughter an animal for him, and such person, due to his own timidity, wounds himself, the person requesting the service must pay 1/3 of the damages (C. of G. T. — 21), etc.

The customs of the Voguls, Ostyaks and Samoyeds permit the same point of view. For the causing of damage by way of a negligent act, e.g. for fire with the loss or damage of things, the author is responsible. But if the loss of the thing lent was accidental, half the value of the thing is awarded, or even nothing is awarded (C. of Voguls — 24).

Kirghiz law places the responsibility on the guilty person; thus Art. 179 of the Cus. of the Kir. states: "For all affairs, besides the payment of the claim or koon, the expenses and losses must be paid by the guilty person". If a dog, ox or some other animal causes damage or even the death of someone, then "for the speechless animal no fine or punishment is inflicted", and only the animal itself is given to the injured party or to his clan (*ibid.* 187). If someone breaks an yurt, structure or some other thing, the guilty person pays the damages and is fined one gown or a horse (*ibid.* 169), etc. But the accidental murderer paid a half koon (85), also the murderer in self defence (*ibid*).

The compensation decreased also in case someone grazes cattle on the meadow of another (or mows down such meadow) he pays half the damages (and the grass which is mowed down is taken away) (170).[103]

---

103 Code of Steppe Laws applies, as a rule, the responsibility in accordance with the principle of fault (*v.* Art. 180-2, 4), but allows in special cases the responsibility in accordance with the principle of causing (Arts. 229, 232, 235).

Succession by law (custom) is a fundamental kind of hereditary succession among the native tribes. Hereditary customs of one tribe differ from that of another tribe but in general the heirs are first of all the children (chiefly the sons), and the wife (or the surviving spouse in general), and if there are none — the grandchildren, brothers and other collateral relatives.

The will appeared here later as a supplement to succession by law. Here it did not reach full development and was permitted with certain limitations. For example, by means of a will it is permitted to distribute the successive portions at one's own (the testator's) discretion among the heirs by law — in particular among the children (*cf.* C. Kir — 207) or to appoint a special portion to any one of the sons (Customs of the Samoyeds, 18) or to give legacies to other relatives, e. g. the grandchildren, nephews, if their fathers-heirs exist (Cust. Tung. Gant. — 24). Only in case there are no heirs by law, it is permitted to will the estate to a member of a strange clan (Cus. Sel. — 133). Even in such case the Customs of the Tunguses require the permission of the clan officials in order to put the will into effect (Cus. of Gant. Tung. 25) because the property thus leaves the clan. The Customs of the Kirhgiz allow to appoint 1/8 of the property to strangers in the form of "commemoration", while the remaining property must go to the heirs by law (206).

We stated elsewhere that succession by law (among the Mongols) arose by virtue of family law from the partition of property during the lifetime of the father among the children and the heirs.[104] We find the confirmation of this point of view in respect to the primitive will in the Customs of the Samoyeds, whereby it is possible "to will to some son in the presence of the clan chief or elder or to do a partition during the lifetime at one's own discretion" (Art. 18, *in fine*). Here also we see the levelling of the partition of property during the lifetime, and hereditary succession.

We allow ourselves to made a few general remarks respecting the legal condition of the aforesaid tribes.

The material which we have examined produces before us a picture of the nomadic, patriarchal clan life with its most important elements (the division into clans, the recognition of relationship through the father, the strong power of the head of the family — the father, the permanent exogamous marriage, the weakness of the

---

104 *v.* Mongol Law, 1931 (in Russ) pg. 302; Fundamental Principles of Mongol Law, 1937 pg. 250-251.

power of the State, a nomadic economy with the absence of the right of ownership over immovables and a weak civil life, etc.). But side by side with a developed patriarchal-clan order we find here considerable survivals of the matriarchate (a special attitude towards the mothers clan, the survivals of the *avunkulat*, the classificatory system of relationship, the levirate and some others). Moreover, we find here a tendency of a number of institutions towards further evolution: the degeneration of the clan, the recognition among several tribes of a close relationship by the mother, the weakening of exogamy, the weakening of polygamy, the modification of the power of the father, and some others. All this provides the ground to conclude that the primary type of social relations among the aforesaid tribes was the matriarchate, which was replaced by the patriarchal-clan order of social relations, and the latter, in its turn, is progressing towards further evolution.

Equally so, on the basis of this material we can arrive at the conclusion that in the sphere of family relations the aforesaid tribes passed through the stage of the matriarchal family with its basic form of marriage — group marriage, and lived through the stage of the patriarchal family with its basic form of marriage — polygamy, and are now approaching the stage of a family with equal mutual rights (an individual family) with its monogamic marriage. The abduction of the bride, the purchase, and the free consent of those engaged to be married are the three basic and consistent forms of marriage here.

In the sphere of property relations we see here a distinction of individual ownership over movable property acquired by one's own labour from the clan and family property; immovable property (with very minor exceptions) remains in the common use of the clan unions, and the development of civil life is insignificant.

In concluding we permit ourselves to note also the following position:

Earlier we studied quite fully the customary law of the Mongol tribes[105], and here we set forth in brief the customary law of a number of the non-Mongol tribes of Siberia (all the tribes named

105 *v.* V. A. Riasanovsky — "Customary Law of the Mongol Tribes", 1929; "Mongol Law with Reference to Customary Law", 1931 (in Russ); Fundamental Principles of Mongol Law, 1937.

in the present outline, with the exception of the Buriats, are of a non-Mongol origin). However, even this brief investigation of the question gives the basis for certain conclusions relative to the juristic culture of the nomadic (Mongol and non-Mongol) tribes of Asia. Let us note this question here quite briefly.

1. First of all it is necessary to note that the presence of one and the same nomadic patriarchal clan culture united not only the tribes of Siberia which we have mentioned here, but also those of Mongolia. The same nomadic patriarchal clan culture lies in the basis of the social organization of the Mongol tribes: the northern Mongols — Khalkas and Buriats, and Western Mongols — Djungars and Kalmucks, as well as the non-Mongol tribes — Kirghiz, Ostyaks, Altais, Tartars, Tunguses, Yakuts and certain others.

2. The community of the culture of the nomadic Mongol and non-Mongol tribes of Asia creates an identity of the fundamental juristic institutions of all these tribes. Among all of them we find the clan organization of the partriarchal type with the clan Court and administration, exogamy, the counting of relationship only by the father, permanent marriages and polygamy, the strong power of the father in the family, but also the survivals of the matriarchate, the weakly developed authority of the State, the absence of the right of ownership over immovables and the using of the latter by the clan units in the interests of the nomadic economy, and the weakly developed civil life.

3. But the study of the customary law of the nomadic tribes of Siberia not only enlightens for us the general picture of the condition of the customary law of the nomadic tribes of Asia (at least of the Central and Western Asia) and confirms our general views on the development of the customary law of the nomadic tribes of Asia as expressed by us in the study of the customary law of the Mongol tribes (*cf.*, *e. g.* Fundamental Principles, Ch. IV, b, c. d, Ch. V *in fine*) but also introduces a number of special details into the picture of this development.

Thus this study shows to us that, firstly, Mongol law had a great influence on the law of the nomadic non-Mongol tribes of Siberia, and not only in the sphere of administration (their conquest by and the inclusion into the Mongol Empire) and the military organization but also in the sphere of civil and criminal law.

Further, it enlightens before us the process of the development of a number of institutions of modern law, e. g. the process of the development of the gratuitous contract of gift from the customs of the clan hospitality, or of the primitive will from the partition of the property by the father among his children during his, the father's, lifetime, or of the degeneration of the blood revenge (e. g. in the institution of the "baranta" among the Kirghiz), etc.

All this is very interesting from the point of view of Comparative Jurisprudence.

But here we shall not go deeper into this question in order not to pass the limits of our object. In the present brief outline we only wanted to enlighten the fundamental characteristics of the badly-investigated customary law of the nomadic tribes of Siberia. We hope (as is stated in the Preface) to return to these questions once again and to give a more detailed investigation. If, however, we shall be unable to do so, we hope that it will be done by the other investigators, as, according to our conviction, the law of the nomadic tribes of Asia (now dying away) deserves, in the interests of science, a deeper study than has been the case until the present.

For Product Safety Concerns and Information please contact our EU
representative GPSR@taylorandfrancis.com
Taylor & Francis Verlag GmbH, Kaufingerstraße 24, 80331 München, Germany

www.ingramcontent.com/pod-product-compliance
Ingram Content Group UK Ltd.
Pitfield, Milton Keynes, MK11 3LW, UK
UKHW020207200926
475702UK00004B/647

* 9 7 8 0 7 0 0 7 0 8 4 8 2 *